And, God, What About . . . ?

AND, GOD,
WHAT ABOUT . . . ?

James T. Cumming
Hans Moll

Art by
Kathy Counts

CPH™
SAINT LOUIS

Concordia Publishing House, St. Louis, Missouri
Copyright © 1980 Concordia Publishing House

MANUFACTURED IN THE UNITED STATES OF AMERICA
6 7 8 9 10 11 12 13   01 00 99 98 97 96 95 94

Library of Congress Cataloging in Publication Data

Cumming, James T   1938—
    And, God, what about . . . ?

    Includes index.
    1. Theology—Miscellanea.   I. Moll, Hans, 1938—
joint author.   II. Title.
BR96.C849   230   80-10401
ISBN 0-570-03806-5

We dedicate this book
to the glory of God
with loving thanks
to our parents,
Alexander and Dorothy Cumming
and
John and Mary Moll

Contents

Preface

To all of our readers "... whom God loves and has called to be His holy people! May God our Father and the Lord Jesus Christ continue to show you grace and give you peace" (Rom. 1:7).

Through the guidance of the Holy Spirit a question-and-answer book has been maintained in the main entrance to the Lutheran Student Center/Chapel of St. Timothy the Learner, Macomb, Ill. This chapel serves the students of Western Illinois University. Students have been encouraged to ask, anonymously, questions that are of concern to them. The questions have all been carefully answered, after prayer, on the basis of the Bible and the Lutheran Confessions.

It was during the 1974 spring quarter that a student came to the campus pastor with a series of questions on Lutheran living and theology. In the course of helping this student search out and answer his questions, the student suggested that others had similar concerns but lacked a convenient and private way of asking their questions. He further suggested that some way be provided so that others could benefit as he had. From these counseling sessions grew the question-and-answer book described above.

The book *Hey, God, What About . . . ?* (Concordia Publishing House, 1977) was based on the questions submitted from March 1974 to July 1976.

This book is based on questions asked since July 1976. In all cases (except for the two "Cathy" cartoons) the questions are the words and thoughts of students.

The purpose of this book is to spread the Gospel of Jesus Christ as it pertains to the daily lives of young adults living in the 1980s.

As in the first book, these questions and their answers can be divided into two major categories, Christian/Lutheran living and Christian/Lutheran theology.

All Bible passages quoted are from *The Holy Bible: An American Translation* (third edition), by William F. Beck, unless otherwise noted.

Thanks to Ed Higginbotham, who first proposed the question-and-answer book for the Lutheran Student Center. Thanks also to the people who provided financial support for the distribution of the first book to appropriate people. For typing we thank Heidi Ann Moll and Linda Smith. Special thanks and love to wives Marcia and Margaret, and our children Amy, Carol, Christine, David, Debra, Emily, and Heidi, and A.F.S. student Sharron Ayre for their support, encouragement, and understanding during the months of preparation.

J.T.C.
H.G.M.

ALPHABETICAL INDEX OF THE BOOKS
OF THE OLD AND NEW TESTAMENTS

Abbreviation	Book	Old Testament	New Testament
Acts	Acts		X
Amos	Amos	X	
1 Chron.	1 Chronicles	X	
2 Chron.	2 Chronicles	X	
Col.	Colossians		X
1 Cor.	1 Corinthians		X
2 Cor.	2 Corinthians		X
Dan.	Daniel	X	
Deut.	Deuteronomy	X	
Eccles.	Ecclesiastes	X	
Eph.	Ephesians		X
Esther	Esther	X	
Ex.	Exodus	X	
Ezek.	Ezekiel	X	
Ezra	Ezra	X	
Gal.	Galatians		X
Gen.	Genesis	X	
Hab.	Habakkuk	X	
Hag.	Haggai	X	
Heb.	Hebrews		X
Hos.	Hosea	X	
Is.	Isaiah	X	
James	James		X
Jer.	Jeremiah	X	
Job	Job	X	
Joel	Joel	X	
John	John		X
1 John	1 John		X
2 John	2 John		X
3 John	3 John		X

Jonah	Jonah	X	
Joshua	Joshua	X	
Jude	Jude		X
Judg.	Judges	X	
1 Kings	1 Kings	X	
2 Kings	2 Kings	X	
Lam.	Lamentations	X	
Lev.	Leviticus	X	
Luke	Luke		X
Mal.	Malachi	X	
Mark	Mark		X
Matt.	Matthew		X
Micah	Micah	X	
Nah.	Nahum	X	
Neh.	Nehemiah	X	
Num.	Numbers	X	
Obad.	Obadiah	X	
1 Peter	1 Peter		X
2 Peter	2 Peter		X
Philem.	Philemon		X
Phil.	Philippians		X
Prov.	Proverbs	X	
Ps.	Psalms	X	
Rev.	Revelation		X
Rom.	Romans		X
Ruth	Ruth	X	
1 Sam.	1 Samuel	X	
2 Sam.	2 Samuel	X	
Song	Song of Solomon	X	
1 Thess.	1 Thessalonians		X

2 Thess.	2 Thessalonians		X
1 Tim.	1 Timothy		X
2 Tim.	2 Timothy		X
Titus	Titus		X
Zech.	Zechariah	X	

| Zeph. | Zephaniah | X | |

BIBLE TRANSLATIONS

KJV	King James Version
NIV	New International Version
RSV	Revised Standard Version

And, God, What About ACCEPTANCE by the Holy Spirit?

 How do you know if the Holy Spirit has accepted you?

Since the Bible is the work of the Holy Spirit, let us begin with the following quotations from Him.

To the praise of the glory of His grace, wherein *He hath made us accepted* in the beloved: In whom we have redemption through His blood, the forgiveness of sins, according to the riches of His grace (Eph. 1:6-7 KJV).

You didn't receive the spirit of slaves to make you feel afraid again, but you received the Spirit who makes us God's children and moves us to call "Abba, Father!" This Spirit assures our spirit we are God's children, and if children, then heirs, God's heirs, who share Christ's inheritance with Him (Rom. 8:15-17).

So I tell you, if you are moved by God's Spirit, you don't say, "Jesus is cursed," and only if you are moved by the Holy Spirit can you say, "Jesus is the Lord" (1 Cor. 12:3).

Anyone who comes to Me I will never turn away (John 6:37b).

On the basis of these passages from the Word of God, I am convinced that everyone who trusts in and confesses Jesus as his or her Lord can be certain that God *has accepted him or her.* As you can see in the first passage, God makes us acceptable to Himself. In the second passage, the Spirit makes us God's children. The Spirit does that through the blood of Jesus. In Jesus alone forgiveness of sin and the grace of God are to be found. When you accept what Jesus offers, then, and only then, can you call God Father (even, affectionately, Dad, "Abba"). When you use such an affectionate form of address, you know that it is the Holy Spirit who has enabled you to do so; the Holy Spirit alone converts us from death in sin to life in Christ. He is the One who moves us to confess Jesus as our personal Savior and Lord. That same Holy Spirit bears an inner testimony to us that we are God's adopted children. As adopted children we can know with certainty that we are accepted by God.

The John 6:37 passage gives unconditional assurance that when we come to Jesus, repenting of our sins and trusting in His mercy and forgiveness, He will not turn us away. He accepts *all* who come to Him.

It is when we live by "every word that God speaks" (Matt. 4:4) that our confidence in the mercy of God grows. It is through the Bible that the Holy Spirit bears witness with our spirit that we have been accepted by God. Therefore we urge you to get into the Word, read the Bible. The more we read and study God's Word, the more deeply we can say with St. Paul:

> Nothing above or below, or any other creature can ever separate us from God, who loves us in Christ Jesus, our Lord (Rom. 8:39).

The above indicates that the Spirit has accepted you when you have accepted Jesus. That is all that is needed. You do not need any extraordinary spiritual experience such as speaking in tongues. The Christian faith is based on the truth of the Word of God, not emotional experiences. (See also the question on speaking in TONGUES.)

Pray with us: "Thank You, God the Father, for the gift of Your Son, who makes us acceptable to You. Thank You for the work of the Holy Spirit in our hearts. Keep us ever in Your way, fill us with the Spirit, and guide us to do Your will, so that in the end we may be brought to Your everlasting salvation. We ask this in the name of Jesus. Amen."

And, God, What About ANGELS?

 Why, if angels have been in heaven since earth began, is there no reference to them in the creation story? I know it says God created heaven and earth, but if the angels were so important to God, why then would He not make mention of their creation?

 Since God has not seen fit to report the creation of the angels to us, nor to explain why He has not done so, I am not able to give a definite answer to your questions. What follows is this Bible student's opinion on the subject of the creation of angels.

I do think that angels were created by God at the same time that the world was created.

> And so the heavens and the earth and *everything* in them were finished (Gen. 2:1).
> *Everything* was made by Him, and not one thing that was made was made without Him (John 1:3).
> In Him was created *everything* you can see and cannot see in heaven and on earth—thrones, lords, rulers, or powers—*everything* was created by Him and for Him (Col. 1:16).

It may be that God has not told us very much about the creation of the angels because He does not want us to pay too much attention to them. He may want us to think of them only in reference to Himself. He certainly does not want us to pray to them or worship them. He does not want us to think of them as intermediaries between Him and us or us and Him. It is possible, then, that God deemphasizes angels.

Have you ever noticed that we are not told that God created the sun and the moon in Gen. 1? What we read in Gen. 1:16 is:

God made two large lights, the larger one to control the day and the smaller one to control the night. . . .

It is obvious what lights are meant. However, the names sun and moon do not appear in the text.

Why is it that the sun and the moon are referred to by their appearance and their function rather than by name? You may know that the sun and the moon have been worshiped as gods. It may be that the Lord God did not want those who read the Bible to get the idea that when He created the sun and the moon He was creating other gods. Angels appear to be deemphasized in the Bible for the same reasons that the sun and the moon are deemphasized in Gen. 1.

There have been people who have regarded angels as emanations of God. They have regarded them as the agents of the remote Creator God. Angels were thus considered intermediaries between God and man— intermediaries who were in control of the material world. As such, angels were regarded as worthy of worship and service. All of this is, of course, too much emphasis on angels.

There are students of the Bible who think that references in the Epistle to the Colossians (1:15-17; 2:8, 15) to the thrones, lords, rulers, and powers are made against the background of angel worship. In those passages a contrast is made between Christ, the fulness of the Godhead in bodily form (Col. 2:9 KJV), and all worldly power. In Col. 2:8 Christians are warned to beware of those who deceive them into following false doctrines.

Our all-wise God anticipated the distortions of His revealed truth. He seems to have seen the consequences of overemphasis on the place of angels in His universe. Therefore He chose not to tell us about their creation.

God has, however, revealed that His angel hosts are ministering spirits who are sent to help those who are going to be saved (Heb. 1:14). Their importance has to do with their service. They serve God and the people of God. They do not give glory to themselves; they give all glory to Him.

In the remainder of this answer I would like to share with you some of the many Bible passages that talk about the fourfold function of angels.

1. They convey messages from God to man.

After the Wise Men left, Joseph in a dream saw the Lord's angel,

who said, "Get up, take the little Child and His mother, and flee to Egypt. Stay there till I tell you. Herod is going to search for the Child to kill Him" (Matt. 2:13).
(See also Gen. 31:11; Matt. 2:19-20; Acts 27:23-24).

2. They were used to foretell special acts of God.

Then the Lord's Angel told her: "You're going to have a child; you'll have a son, and you'll call him Ishmael because the Lord heard your cry of distress" (Gen. 16:11).
(See also Judg. 13:3-5; Luke 1:11-20, 26-38; 2:9-12).

3. They execute God's judgment.

Immediately the Lord's angel struck him because he didn't give glory to God. He was eaten by worms, and he died (Acts 12:23).
(See also Gen. 19:1, 11; 2 Sam. 24:15-17; Matt. 13:41-42, 49-50.)

4. They serve as agents of divine providence.

He orders His angels to be with you and protect you everywhere you go. They will carry you in their hands and not let you stub your foot against a stone (Ps. 91:11-12).
(See also 1 Kings 19:5-8; Dan. 6:22; Acts 5:19; 12:7.)

The Bible does not clearly state that each of us has a personal guardian angel. However, Jesus says:

Be careful not to despise one of these little ones. I tell you their angels in heaven always see the face of My Father in heaven (Matt. 18:10).

In summary, angels are messengers of God. They are used by God for many purposes. They were created by God to serve Him and His people.

And, God, Why Don't You Create ANOTHER SON?

If God is all-powerful, why doesn't He create another Son to share His message with the world?

As a follower of Jesus I believe that God is all-powerful and that He can do whatever He pleases. The ultimate answer to your question lies with Him alone. The answer that follows is based on what God has chosen to reveal to us in the Bible.

In the Bible we are told that Jesus is *the* only way into the presence of God. No one comes to God the Father except through Jesus (John 14:6b). There is salvation in only one name, the name of Jesus (Acts 4:12). God's message of repentance and forgiveness of sins is to be preached to all people in Jesus' name (Luke 24:47).

This is true because Jesus said on the cross:

It is finished! (John 19:30a).

That does not mean that Jesus was finished. The "it" that Jesus finished was His assignment of redeeming all people from sin and death. When Jesus said, "It is finished" (*tetelestai*), He was stating that all the sins (the moral debts) of mankind were paid in full. *Tetelestai* has been found written across the face of ancient bills exactly as you find "Paid in full" stamped today. Hence, if Jesus finished the job, it is not necessary to send anyone else ("another Son" as you suggest) to do any more.

Sharing the Good News of the full payment of our moral debts is now the privilege and responsibility of those who trust in Jesus. In a very real sense God creates us as His sons and daughters when He brings us to faith in Jesus (see John 1:12-13). As sons and daughters of God, our major responsibility is to share freely what God in Christ has shared with us. The Christians who built and maintain this building did so because they take seriously this responsibility of sharing God's love. They want to be wise unto the salvation which is in Christ Jesus. Are you that wise?

And, God, What About Dying Without BAPTISM?

The Bible says: "Believe and be baptized and you shall be saved." What happens in a case of an infant who is too young to believe and the parents haven't had the time to get it* baptized? For instance, it* dies immediately after birth.

"I will tell you the truth," Jesus answered him, "if anyone isn't born of water and the Spirit, he can't get into God's kingdom" (John 3:5).

From the above the Christian is obligated to say that Baptism is necessary for salvation and entry into God's kingdom.

The Christian church, Christian people, and Christian ministers cannot take exception to this "rule" which God Himself has established for us.

Hence, the first answer to your question would indicate that an unbaptized infant would not "get into God's kingdom."

That said, we are aware that the Maker of the rule may make an exception to the rule. The classic example of an exception to the rule that we are to believe *and* be baptized is the repentant thief who was crucified with Jesus. Most certainly this man was not baptized before he died. After he turned to Jesus in repentance and faith, Jesus said to him:

Today you will be with Me in Paradise" (Luke 23:43).

We may cautiously apply this exception to the rule to children who die before they are baptized. The Lutheran Church has always held that "not the lack but only the contempt of Baptism damns." Moreover, Christian couples who are awaiting the birth of a baby will intercede with our Father in heaven on behalf of their prebirth child's well-being, and God has promised to hear the fervent prayers of righteous persons. So hope can be offered to the parents of the child who dies without the benefit of Christian Baptism.

At times those who raise questions about the necessity of Baptism and particularly the Baptism of children do so because they think that children do not need the blessings of Holy Baptism. Some people think that somehow children are conceived and born without sin. That notion, however, is clearly contrary to the Scriptures, which say:

Yes, I was born guilty, and when my mother conceived me I was in sin (Ps. 51:5).

And,

Anything born of the flesh is flesh (John 3:6).

Man's natural depravity, called original sin, is one of the "hard" teachings of the Bible. It is hard for us to take, but it points out the absolute need every human being who has ever lived, lives, or will live has for the grace of God. That grace He has provided in Jesus Christ. John 3:16 tells us:

God so loved the *world* that He gave His only-begotten Son. . . .

"The world" includes every human being. Children are most certainly human beings. When the apostle Peter preached on Pentecost, he urged those who responded to his heartrending sermon to repent and to be baptized in the name of Jesus. He said that via their Baptism they would receive the forgiveness of their sins and the gift of the Holy

Spirit. He also said that the promise of God's grace was for them and for their *children* (Acts 2:37-39). When the apostle Paul baptized Lydia and the jailer in Philippi, he baptized their whole households, all who were with them (Acts 16:13-34). Therefore we conclude that children need and can benefit from the means of grace which is Holy Baptism. Praise God that He wants the young children brought to Him! (Mark 10:13-16).

*Permit us to make the following observation and suggestions about the use of "it" when referring to a human being. A human infant is certainly not an "it"; he or she is a boy or a girl. From the very instant of conception a human is either a male or a female. Please do not play into the hands of those who deny the humanity of the newborn and/or the prebirth human being by calling the child "it." When you realize that the principle of the sanctity of human life is at stake, you will find it easy to always speak of "he or she" when you refer to the prebirth child.

And, God, What About Spiritual BLAHS?

Q *Pastor: I guess you could say I have a very common problem. A lot of times I am not sure I am really in a good relationship with God. My Quiet Time (when I have it) is sort of blah, as if I don't feel the Holy Spirit nudging me or convicting me when I sin. I don't feel that my walk (or should I say limp?) with God is routine. But I have so much trouble disciplining myself in having a Quiet Time.*

A Your insight about yourself and your spiritual relationship with God is the first step in realizing that you need God's help. Such a realization is necessary because the source of spiritual development is not in *ourselves* but in *God.* Unlike many popular philosophies of our day, God in His Word does not direct us into ourselves. He directs us to Someone else. He directs us to Jesus.

Unlike Transcendental Meditation or any of the other forms of meditation that are not "of God/Christ," Quiet Time for the Christian is not a time when we "empty" ourselves or concentrate on something that is meaningless. The Christian will want his or her meditation (Quiet Time) to be upon God, upon His Word, and upon His wondrous works and ways. The Christian will want to be filled with God. God fills us when we read the Bible. We suggest you read one of the modern translations of the Bible. The King James Version may seem hard to understand because of the old form of the English language. *Only* by continuing to read Jesus' Word can we know the truth and be freed from the sin that clings so closely to us (John 8:31-32; Heb. 12:1 RSV).

It was through hearing the message of Christ that you were made alive in Him, and so, logically, it is only by remaining in the Word that you can grow in grace and in the knowledge of Christ. If you are reading the Word, you can be certain that He will convict you when you sin. You can also be certain that God loves you, will forgive your sins, be with you now, and finally take you to heaven.

Therefore I murmur not,
Heaven is my home;
Whate'er my earthly lot,
Heaven is my home;
And I shall surely stand
There at my Lord's right hand.
Heaven is my fatherland,
Heaven is my home.

The Lutheran Hymnal, 660:4

And, God, What About Christian CARING?

 I have had a great deal of trouble thru my lifetime, but with the help of God I am strong enough to handle it. I only wish I knew of someone to talk to like you. It seems in today's society no one really cares about other people . . . only themselves. I can tell that you do care, and I really admire you for that. You must be a wonderful person! Thank God!

Someone else who cares

 As explained in the preface of this book, the statement above was written in a public place, a university student chapel. Before I even saw the question, three different students had written:

"I care. Don"

"I care. Jesus"

"I care!! Nancy"

Don even gave his address and phone number in an attempt to reach a person troubled by an uncaring society. I am touched by these responses and thank the Holy Spirit for them.

I am convinced that when we Christians really know the love of God in Jesus, we will want to share it with others since it is too good to hoard.

Thank you for your kind words, but understand that all glory belongs to God.

And, God, What About CATHOLIC?

If "Catholic" means "universal," then does this mean to say that the Catholic Church really was the first church? If so, did the Catholic Church get corrupt and is that why Martin Luther split away?

The word "catholic" can be defined as "universal." The 1968 edition of *Webster's New World Dictionary,* page 232, offers the following etymology and definitions for the adjective "catholic."

[From Latin, *catholicus,* universal, general; from Greek, *katholikos, kata,* down, completely + *holos,* whole],
1. universal; all-inclusive; of general interest or value; hence,
2. having broad sympathies or understanding; liberal.
3. of the universal Christian church; of the Christian church as a whole.
4. [C-], of the Western (Roman) Christian Church as dinstinguished from the Eastern (Orthodox) Christian Church; hence,
5. [C-], of the Christian church headed by the Pope; Roman Catholic.
6. [C-], of any of the orthodox Christian churches, including the Roman, Greek Orthodox, and Anglo-Catholic, as distinguished from the Reformed or Protestant churches.

The adjective "catholic," hence, has several meanings and has been used in many ways over the years. In order to answer your question as to whether what is known today as the Catholic Church is the "first church," one must dig into the history of the use of the term.

The earliest use of the term "Catholic Church" appears to be in a letter written by Ignatius, Bishop of Antioch in Syria (early second century), to the Christians at Smyrna. It is thought that Ignatius died as a martyr for Christ during the Roman emperor Trajan's reign (A.D. 98—117). The following is the sentence that is of interest:

Where the bishop is present, there let the congregation gather; just as where Jesus Christ is, there is the Catholic Church (Richardson, C.C., ed., *Early Christian Fathers* [Philadelphia: Westminster, 1953], p. 115).

At the beginning of the second century the term "bishop" was applied to the pastor of a local congregation. The expression does not suggest that he presided over a diocese. The church organization of dioceses came later. In the *Letter to the Smyrnaeans,* Ignatius is obviously writing of the contrast between the bishop presiding over a local congregation and Jesus, the Shepherd and Bishop of our souls, presiding over all Christians and all congregations of Christians. There is no identification of the Catholic Church of Ignatius with a church headquartered at Rome. In fact, it is interesting to note that Ignatius was hauled off to Rome and thrown to the lions in the Coliseum for his faith and loyalty to Christ. At the beginning of the second century Rome was not the seat of Christian authority.

Another early use of the term "Catholic Church" is found in the Letter of the Church in Smyrna to the Church of Philomelium. This letter is commonly called the *Martyrdom of Polycarp,* because of its subject matter. Polycarp was bishop of Smyrna and was burned at the stake for his faith in Jesus in the middle of the second century. In 8:1 of the text of the *Martyrdom of Polycarp* one reads:

> When at last he [Polycarp] had finished his prayer, in which he remembered all who had met with him at any time, both small and great, both those with and those without renown, and the *whole Catholic Church throughout the world,* the hour of departure having come, they mounted him on an ass and brought him into the city (Ibid., pp. 151—152).

Toward the end of this important document there are other references to the Catholic Church. In each case it is clear that the reference is to the church into which all who trust in Jesus are called and gathered.

In early documents quoted by Henry Bettenson in his work *Documents of the Christian Church* (New York: Oxford University Press, 1960), pp. 22—24, it is interesting to note the references to the church. In the "Edict of Toleration" of 311 issued by Galerius and bearing the names of the Roman emperors Constantine and Licinius, reference is made only to "the Christians." Then in the "Edict of Milan" of March 313 Constantine and Licinius refer to "Christians" and "churches." However, later in 313 Constantine wrote a letter to Anulinus, proconsul of Africa, in which he asked that Anulinus see to it that property belonging "to the Catholic Church of Christians" be restored. Also in 313 Constantine wrote to Caecilian, bishop of Carthage, about the granting of subsidy "to certain specified ministers of the legitimate and most holy Catholic religion."

It is evident that the term "Catholic" has not always been used. When it was first used, it referred to the broader-than-local fellowship of followers of Jesus.

The development of what we today call the Apostles' Creed also reveals how the term "Catholic" was introduced. The Old Roman Creed is thought to have been delivered by Marcellus, bishop of Ancyra, to Julius, bishop of Rome, around the year 340. Its tenth statement of faith is: "I believe in . . . the holy church . . ." (ibid., p. 34).

Following almost an identical format, Caesarius, Bishop of Arles

(503—43), confessed in a Gallican Creed of the sixth century: "I believe in the Holy Ghost, the Holy Catholic Church, the communion of saints" (ibid., p. 35). Hence, we can see that the church, to which allegiance was sworn, was considered holy, catholic, and "the communion of saints."

In 380 Emperor Theodosius I (379—95) in his *Cunctos populos* authorized that those who confess that there is one God who is the Father, the Son, and the Holy Spirit, who are in equal majesty and in a Holy Trinity, be called "Catholic Christians." Those who do not thus confess the Christian faith were to be considered heretics. In 381 in his *Nullus haereticus* Theodosius wrote of his desire that "the Catholic churches throughout the world may be restored to the orthodox bishops who hold the faith of Nicaea" (Ibid., p. 32).

It is not until page 100 in his *A History of Christianity* that Kenneth Scott Latourette writes of "Catholics." He does so in contrast to the Arians. The Arians, the followers of Arius, were condemned at the Council of Nicaea (A.D. 325) for their teaching that Jesus is not fully God, that He is only of similar substance to the Father, and that there was a time when He was not. The Nicene Creed condemns such notions with the terse statement that Jesus is "of one substance with the Father." Church historian Latourette thus begins to use the expression "Catholic Christianity" to distinguish it from the heterodox teaching of the Arians. Again, by such a use Latourette is not referring to the Roman Catholic Church.

It is clearly a matter of historical development that in time the headquarters of the Catholic Church became Rome. That does not mean that the churches of the Eastern Roman Empire, which were called Orthodox churches, did not subscribe to the Catholic faith. It is obvious in the early uses of the term "catholic" that it was used interchangeably with "Christian" and "orthodox."

Hence, "Catholic" means the universal community of true believers and should not be used as a synonym for "Roman Catholic Church."

Let me answer the second part of your question rather briefly. There is general agreement that prior to the Reformation of the 16th century there was a great deal of corruption within the church which had its headquarters in Rome. Concerned Christians challenged what was going on within the church of Rome for more than 100 years before Martin Luther.

In England, John Wyclif (1328—84) raised the cry for reform. In Prague, Jan Hus (c. 1373—1415) raised his voice. In Italy, Girolamo Savonarola (1452—98) raised his voice. For their efforts all of these men were condemned by the Roman Catholic Church. Although Wyclif died a natural death on the last day of 1384, the Council of Constance in 1415 condemned him on 260 counts and ordered that his bones be exhumed and cast out of consecrated ground. It was that same Council of Constance that condemned Jan Hus and ordered him burned at the stake for his "heresy." Savonarola was condemned, hung, and his body burned in the great piazza of Florence in 1498.

Then God raised up Martin Luther. He was born in 1483. He challenged the sale of indulgences in 1517 with his *Ninety-Five Theses*. He was excommunicated in 1521. Unlike Wyclif, Hus, and Savonarola before him, Luther was given a great deal of support by powerful people; so he was not eliminated. He also had the help of the recently invented printing press. He was an advocate of reform in the church; but the organized church would not listen, and so it expelled him. Expelling Luther did not silence him. Many people rallied to his side, studied the Scriptures with him, and professed with him the truths of the Bible which point to Jesus Christ as our sole Redeemer from all sin.

Martin Luther raised his voice in such a way that he was no longer welcome within the fold of the Roman Church. Luther's contemporary Desiderius Erasmus (1455—1536) also raised his voice. He also called for reform, but he did not go so far that he was excommunicated. The Catholic or Counter Reformation, which followed the Protestant Reformation, surely is evidence that there was a need for reform in the Roman Catholic Church. No Roman Catholic authority today will deny that there was serious corruption in the church at the time when Luther and others raised their cries for reformation.

In closing, it should be noted that Martin Luther began as a reformer of the Roman Catholic Church. He began his work out of love for God and the church, not out of hate. Only after his excommunication did he begin to lead a new church body. That church body's teaching is based on the principle that the Bible is the sole basis for making us wise to salvation through faith in Christ Jesus and for training us in right living (2 Tim. 3:15-17). (See also the question on the FIRST CHURCH.)

And, God, What About Not Going to CHURCH?

 I haven't been to church in over three years. Is it possible to receive God without having to go to church? I do believe in Him.

 Faith in God is dynamic, not static. Faith in God never stays the same; it either grows or shrinks. If you do not feed your faith, it will weaken just as you will weaken when you do not feed your body. We live in a world that laughs at anyone who lives by faith. There are many people and things which would tear down your faith. Do you think your faith in God is as strong today as it was three years ago?

Do you think God loves you as strongly as He did three years ago?

Permit this little analogy. For over three years you have not heard a loved one tell you that he or she loves you. During the same period of time you have not said or expressed your love for that person. In fact, you have not even talked about that love. What do you think will happen to this love which is not shared? How convincing do you think you will be when you start to talk about love after the three years of not doing so?

The analogy is not perfect; analogies never are. I hope, however, that the point is not too sharp.

I am convinced that our trust (or faith) in God is a response to the love He has lavished upon us in Christ Jesus. I cannot speak of faith in God without thinking and meaning trust in Jesus as my personal Savior from all sin. Since I am a sinful man, I need to hear over and over again that God loves me. I hear that in worship services where the Word of God is preached in its truth, purity, and power. In the same worship service I need to respond to God's love letters to me—to respond with prayers, psalms, hymns, and spiritual songs. I need also to know that I am not alone, that others know the same love of God in Jesus and are singing His praises with me. With such needs and such joy, I look forward to the Lord's Day and other opportunities I have to worship with my fellow believers in Christ.

You are welcome to join us, as I am certain you would be welcome anywhere that Christians gather for worship. We say, "Come, join us in the Son!" Break your three-year fast and again dine with God in church (see Rev. 3:20).

To Thy temple I repair;
Lord, I love to worship there
When within the veil I meet
Christ before the mercy seat.

From Thy house when I return,
May my heart within me burn,
And at evening let me say,
"I have walked with God today."

The Lutheran Hymnal, 2:1, 7

And, God, What About Close COMMUNION?

In the Bible it teaches that it is possible for a person to eat and drink judgment on himself in Communion. I understand that the Lutheran practice of close Communion attempts to prevent this, but why is Communion restricted solely to Lutherans and not to all who profess a belief in the presence of the body and blood with the bread and wine?

Attendance at Lutheran celebrations of the Lord's Supper implies a three-level commitment to Christ. We believe that communi-

28

cants must be Christians, must accept the Real Presence of Christ's body in the bread and His blood in the wine, and must share oneness of faith and doctrine. In the remainder of this answer we will expand on each of these three points which, when taken together, we call "close Communion."

1. *Being a Christian*

When Jesus first celebrated the Lord's Supper, the only people in attendance were His disciples. The Lord's Supper does not bring people to faith in Jesus. It sustains and nourishes the faith in Him that they already have. Hence, one must be a Christian to attend Holy Communion.

2. *Accepting the Real Presence*

Jesus states forthrightly: "This is My body" and "This is My blood of the covenant" (Matt. 26:26, 28). Concerning the Lord's Supper the apostle Paul asks the leading questions: "Is the cup of blessing which we bless not a communion of the blood of Christ? Is the bread which we break not a communion of the body of Christ?" (1 Cor. 10:16). Paul also wrote that it is possible to profane the Lord's body and blood and to eat and drink judgment upon oneself if one goes to the Lord's Supper not discerning the Lord's body (1 Cor. 11:27-29).

On the basis of these passages, we Lutherans do not think that Jesus was using a figure of speech when He spoke the Words of Institution for Holy Communion. Although we do not understand *how* the bread and the wine can be Jesus' body and blood, we feel obligated to take Jesus at His word. Hence, we teach the Real Presence of Jesus' true body and blood in the Lord's Supper. We expect those who commune with us to believe in the Real Presence. Our close Communion practice is designed to protect people from eating and drinking judgment upon themselves at our altars. Many Christians will agree with this position concerning the Real Presence of the body and blood of Christ in the celebration of the Lord's Supper. However, these Christians may hold membership in congregations and church bodies which do not believe, teach, and confess the Real Presence. This brings us to the third point.

3. *Sharing Oneness of Faith and Doctrine*

Lutherans consider communing together to be a testimony to the oneness of faith and doctrine that exists among those who commune. We do not think the Lord's Supper is properly used as a means of achieving unity of doctrine between various church bodies.

This is not to say that we do not desire oneness of doctrine, for we read: "Make me very happy—be one in thought and in love, live in harmony, keep one purpose in mind" (Phil. 2:2).

In our circles, attendance at the Lord's Table is considered one of the privileges of church membership. Such membership is entered into after basic instruction in Biblical teaching as believed and confessed by the Lutheran Church. This study is followed by public acceptance of the oneness of faith and doctrine in a church rite called confirmation.

Since we do not regard participation in the Lord's Supper as necessary for salvation, our close Communion procedure does not prevent people from going to heaven. It is designed, however, to insure that no one will eat and drink judgment upon himself at the Lord's Table in our midst and to preserve the testimony to the unity of faith and doctrine that we feel the Lord's Supper should be.

And, God, I'm CONFUSED!

Hi! My life right now is filled with a lot of unhappiness. I've tried putting everything into God's hands, but I feel no relief—things just get rougher. I think in Matthew somewhere where Jesus talks to the people and He says blessed are the . . . blessed are the . . . for they shall . . . and so forth, then it says something about "Blessed are the pure in heart." I hope I'm assuming right what pure in heart means—example, David in the Old Testament committed adultery, killed, sin period; but God knew David's inner thought, just thoughts, his heart was pure; God called him a man of God. With all my problems I feel like calling it quits. I am a sincere believer in Christ, I really try to be a good Christian, I feel God knows my weakness, and I feel He will forgive me for all my sins. Do you know if God forgives you for taking a life? Looking at David He does; God knows what my heart feels for the Lord Jesus Christ. You may think I'm wrong for thinking this way, but only God is my judge. God does forgive if you are truly sorry, doesn't He??????? See ya later in heaven, if not sooner.

I am sorry that you feel so bad. I would like very much to help and comfort you with the same comfort with which God comforts me. I have borrowed that expression from 2 Cor. 1:3-4. Read 2 Cor. 1:3-7 and you will see that God "never promised us a rose garden." In this passage He tells us of the troubles of this life, but then He quickly assures us that He will never leave us or forsake us. Nothing can separate us from the love of God in Christ Jesus (see Rom. 8:38-39). I paraphrase these Bible passages for you because I believe they are the Word of God. When we feel troubled, we should trust only God's Word, not our feelings. God does not lie; He is true to His Word.

I cannot agree with your notion that one can have a pure heart while involved in committing adultery, murder, or suicide (self-murder). I think you are mistaken when you think that the Lord considered David a man of God when he was caught in the slavery of his own sinful desires. It was before he committed adultery and murder that David was called a man after the Lord's heart. It was after David fell down before God in deep and true repentance that God again considered him His

30

child. Neither God nor David were permissive about sin. Look at Psalms 51 and 130 and you will see how repentant David was. Note the tone of these excerpts from each Psalm:

> O God, You are so kind—be merciful to me, Your love is so great—wipe out my wrong; wash me thoroughly from my guilt, and cleanse me from my sin. I realize the wrong I've done, and my sin is always before me. I sinned against You, against You only, and did what is wrong in Your sight (Ps. 51:1-4).
>
> Out of the depths I call You, Lord. Lord, listen to me calling; let Your ears be alert to hear my plea. If You remembered sins, Lord, who could survive? But You forgive us to have us fear You (Ps. 130:1-4).

David, who expresses himself in the passages quoted above, could hardly be thought of as condoning his sin or justifying himself. Rather, he laments his self-enslavement to sin and throws himself on the Savior for liberation from this enslavement.

When you accept the liberation from sin, death, and the power of the devil that Jesus gives you, you do not excuse your lapses into sin. Though you are not perfect and do sin, sin is not your lord; sin no longer has dominion over you. As a Christian, Jesus is your Lord, and it is under His gracious and merciful dominion that you live. A Christian is one who daily seeks the assistance of the Lord in order to live a life that is pleasing to Him. We know what is pleasing to God from what He has revealed to us in the Bible. The Ten Commandments are a summary of what is pleasing to God. The Ten Commandments make it clear that murder (which includes suicide), adultery (which includes fornication for the unmarried), stealing, lying, coveting, etc., are contrary to His will.

In fact, there are strong words in the New Testament that make it clear that

> No murderer has everlasting life remaining in him (1 John 3:15)

and,

> Outside are the dogs and people who do witchcraft, sin sexually, murder, worship idols, and everyone who loves lies and tells them (Rev. 22:15).

It is very unwise to think that once you know the love of God in Christ you cannot commit a faith-destroying sin. The New Testament makes it clear that you can drive the Holy Spirit out of your life. Christians are warned:

> Don't put out the fire of the Spirit (1 Thess. 5:19)

and

Don't grieve God's Holy Spirit (Eph. 4:30).

The way one puts out the fire, grieves, or drives the Spirit out of one's heart and life is by doing those sins listed in Rev. 22:15 and similar passages.

Rather than depend on your own feelings, you need to depend on God's promises and the leading of God's Spirit. It is in and through the Bible that God leads and guides us. It is through His holy Word that God assures us that:

In every way we are hard pressed but not crushed, in doubt but not in despair; hunted but not forsaken; struck down but not destroyed (2 Cor. 4:8-9).

That is what God promises us. When we trust in such a God, we want to do what pleases Him; and we know that nothing can separate us from His great, eternal love.

Abide with me! Fast falls the eventide;
The darkness deepens; Lord, with me abide.
When others helpers fail and comforts flee,
Help of the helpless, oh, abide with me!

Hold Thou Thy cross before my closing eyes,
Shine through the gloom, and point me to the skies.
Heaven's morning breaks, and earth's vain shadows flee;
In life, in death, O Lord, abide with me!

The Lutheran Hymnal, 552:1, 8

And, God, What About CONTINUING in the Word?

 I do have one slight question that maybe you can help me answer. I have eight years of parochial schooling. When I reached high school I completely lost interest in churchgoing, to my mother's dismay. . . . To this day I am not a regular churchgoer. I pray, not for what I want but because I am just thinking about God. Pastor, I was wondering if you could tell me how I would look in the eyes of the Lord from your point of view? Is churchgoing on a regular basis really essential to having a meaningful life with God?

 The first thing you must do is assess your personal relationship with God. In order to do that you should ask yourself, "What does

Jesus mean to me?" That is an important question, because only when you recognize your sins, are sorry that they caused Jesus' death on the cross, and then accept Jesus as your Savior are you right "in the eyes of the Lord." Only the person who believes and trusts in God pleases Him (Heb. 11:6). Such a person delights in the Lord, serves Him with gladness, and enjoys a meaningful life with God.

It is when you know what great things God in Christ has done for you that you cannot keep such good news to yourself. You do not want to keep it to yourself because you realize that others have experienced the same forgiveness, healing, joy, and peace that you have experienced. So you respond to God's grace in worship. You worship God with your fellow Christians. That's what is involved in corporate worship (usually called "church").

From a Lutheran/Reformation point of view one does not attend church services to make Brownie points with God. God does not keep a chart of our nonattendance or attendance. We do not earn favor with God nor do we get to heaven just by going to church. We don't get to heaven by our own effort at all. Rather, Jesus Christ has done it all for us. We do understand that we need each other. In these latter days we need to help each other live by faith in Christ. It is not easy to live for Jesus in a world gone mad with booze, drugs, so-called free love, etc. We need the admonition of the Letter to the Hebrews:

> Let us not stay away from our worship services, as some are regularly doing, but let us encourage one another, all the more because you see the day coming nearer (Heb. 10:25).

I see the worship service as an opportunity to feed on the Word of God and the Lord's Supper. I also see it as an opportunity to build up others and to be built up in my trust in Jesus. I cannot see how anyone can live spiritually without feeding his or her faith. Jesus Himself clearly states:

> If you live in My Word, you are really My disciples, and you will know the truth, and the truth will free you (John 8:31b-32).

Please note that Jesus uses the word "if." He has established this as the condition of discipleship. If you want to be His disciple, you must continue in His Word. Living or continuing in His Word includes reading the Bible and discussing your findings with your fellow Christians. Living in His Word means knowing the truth and being free from the chains of sin.

And, God, Who CREATED You?

 Q *If God created the earth, who created God? Or what and where is His original coming into being?*

A Simply put, no one created God. No one could. As God, He is the Source and the Sustainer of all things. All things owe their existence to Him. If someone created God, then He would not be the Source of everything. It is simply not logical to postulate a source behind the original source of all things.

The very name of God reveals a great deal to us about His self-sufficiency. We read that Moses asked God:

> When I go to Israel and I tell them, "The God of your fathers sends me to you," and they ask me, "What is His name?" what should I answer them? (Ex. 3:14).

God then told Moses:

> Tell Israel, "I AM sends me to you" (Ex. 3:14b).

The name of God is transliterated from the original Hebrew into English characters as YHWH, traditionally pronounced "Jehovah." It means "I AM." God's name reveals to us that He is, that He has always been, and that He will always be. He is forever the same. He is without beginning or end. He is eternal. He is in a class all by Himself. He is completely self-sufficient. He does not depend, for His existence, upon anyone or anything else.

God's eternal nature is beyond our ability to fully comprehend. He has, however, revealed Himself to us in Jesus. In Jesus, Jehovah has made Himself known to us as a God who is gracious and full of mercy.

Is it possible that your question arises from the contemporary naturalistic and evolutionistic mind-set? If so, consider the following from *Time* magazine:

> According to the *Book of Genesis,* the universe began in a single, flashing act of creation; the divine intellect willed all into being, *ex nihilo.* It is not surprising that scientists have generally stayed clear of the question of ultimate authorship, of the final "uncaused cause." In years past, in fact, they held to the Aristotelian idea of a universe that was "ungenerated and indestructible," with an infinite past and an infinite future. This was known as the Steady State theory.

However, the article continues:

> Most astronomers now accept the theory that the universe had an instant of creation, that it came to be in a vast fireball explosion 15 or 20 billion years ago. . . . The so-called Big Bang theory makes some astronomers acutely uncomfortable, even while it ignites in many religious minds a small thrill of confirmation. Reason: The Big Bang theory sounds very much like the story that the Old Testament has been telling all along. (*Time*, Feb. 5, 1979, p. 149)

The Steady State theory fits together with both the ancient notion of the eternity of matter and the modern theory of evolution. It fits because if one is a consistent evolutionist, then one must hold that things have always been evolving. Therefore the theory of evolution cannot be used to explain the origin of all things.

Creation, however, does explain the origin of all things. God, the "uncaused cause," called the universe into being in an instant and has upheld it by His all-powerful Word ever since. To Him we give glory, in Jesus' name.

And, God, What About DIFFICULTIES with People?

 Hi. You know I've been coming to this place and reading this book for some time, and I never thought I'd ever ask any questions. Well, this is it.—How does one learn to get along with people? I like people a lot and have good times with my friends—except a lot of times I clash with them, and it's been happening a lot lately. I've been sitting here for two hours now trying to figure out what my problem is. I must be doing something wrong. All three of my roommates are mad at me. The way I see it, it must be me if all three agree I was out of line—even though right now I don't understand how I was. I guess maybe I'm being hardheaded or feeling sorry for myself—all I know is I'm feeling rotten with myself. I was thinking about going into the argument but that wouldn't be cool, and since you wouldn't be getting both sides of the story it wouldn't be fair to set you up as a judge. I realize they must have a different side to the story or there wouldn't be a conflict—I guess I'm just having problems seeing it completely. I say completely because I told them I could see some of their points but not all of them. They couldn't see any of mine—considering that the whole thing was over something trivial, I feel there must be something more. I feel a kind of resentment from them, I guess you could call it. I enjoy being

by myself sometimes and getting back in tune with me. A lot of people get very upset—they say everybody needs people and say there must be something wrong with me to want to be by myself, or they ask me how it is I don't get lonely. Is it wrong for me to like to be by myself? Well, thanx for listening.

A There is certainly nothing wrong with wanting to be by yourself and enjoying solitude. If, however, you frequently have problems when you are with people, then there is something wrong.

When two or more humans have to live and/or work together for extended periods of time, there will be differences of opinion. How these differences are overcome is more important than the fact that there are differences. If people do not handle their differences amicably, then you have all the ingredients for a bad scene.

If you feel as badly as you indicate, you should tell your roommates how you *feel*. Then ask them what they *feel* you have done wrong. Ask them to be honest about their *feelings*. Then accept their *feelings*, even if you don't agree with them. It is natural to defend yourself; but as you have found, that leads to arguments. You may have found out already that you can win the argument but lose the friend. If you listen and can understand what is bothering your friends, then tell them that you are sorry. Don't say you are sorry if you are not. But if you are sorry, then ask your friends what you and they can do to work and live together amicably.

As a Christian, I accept the biblical teaching that I am sinful. Since I sin, I am not surprised that people get upset with me. I am certain that I have hurt those I have loved. I know that I have not lived up to the expectations others have of me. Even when my intentions were proper, I am certain that I have been misunderstood. It is obvious to me, from the way certain things have gone, that I have been selfish and self-centered in my dealings with others. For all such, I am very sorry; from my God and from those I have hurt, I beg forgiveness.

Forgiveness from God and other people is certainly not something that I or any sinner deserves. It is, however, something that we most definitely need. The Holy Spirit, through the Holy Scriptures, has convinced me that Jesus Christ has fulfilled that need. Jesus is my Forgiveness and my Life. Just as God, through Jesus, has forgiven my sins, I will forgive those who sin against me. The Lord's Prayer says the same thing:

Forgive us our sins, as we, too, forgive everyone who sins against us (Luke 11:4a).

Now, how can you change your behavior so that you can live in greater harmony with your friends? You are on the correct path, since you took the time to think about the latest problem. I am particularly

impressed with your insight that I could not judge the conflict between you and your friends without hearing both sides.

Specifically I would suggest that you examine the problem and put it into one of three categories.

Category 1—Attitudes and opinions. Was the problem such that you all had different opinions or attitudes toward a given subject? If so, you should remember that as unique human beings we all have unique opinions. In most cases you should share opinions, but it is best not to try to change the opinions of others, as we tend to feel that our opinions are as good as anyone's.

Category 2—Method of doing something. Was the problem one where you wanted to go to hamburger restaurant A while they wanted hamburger restaurant B? Or did you argue over putting the wastebasket on the left side of the door while they wanted it on the right side? If you always want things your way in these small matters, then your friends may have a valid reason for being unhappy with you. By small matters, I mean those things which will make no difference two years from now.

Category 3—Morals. Was the question one of doing something not in harmony with your Christian faith? If it was, then you have every right, yes, even a clear command of God, to resist anything that would conflict with your Christian faith. You should resist at all costs, even at the cost of broken friendships.

So, where would you put the problem? If it is in Category 1 or 2, you should be prepared to work with and accept a balance and blend of your wants, needs, desires, and opinions with those of your friends. In other words, bend a little. If you put the problem in Category 3, stick to your Christian faith and morals and do what is correct in the sight of God.

I would encourage you to take advantage of the grace of God in Christ. With the help of God, you will be able to work through the problems you mention. No problem is too hard for God to solve.

And, God, Why Do You Permit Terminal DISEASE?

 If God is all-powerful, why does He allow things like terminal disease to take lives?

 As one who trusts in the mercy of God toward us in Christ Jesus, I also believe that God is all-powerful (omnipotent). This finite human being, however, does not presume to dictate how the infinite God should use His power. I see abundant evidence of the power of God in the universe, and I say with the psalmist:

The heavens are telling how wonderful God is, and the sky announces what His hands have made (Ps. 19:1).

Witnessing the power of God in nature moves me to awe, but does not move me to put my trust in Him or to love Him. I trust God only when I realize that He can be trusted. I love God only when I realize that He first loved me. Such trust and love come into my heart only when I realize that Jesus was willing to die the death I deserved. Jesus suffered "under Pontius Pilate," but He suffered and died *for* me and my sin and the sins of all people. In Jesus I know that absolutely nothing, which includes *suffering and death*, can separate me from the love of God (see Rom. 8:38-39). It is with this conviction that I try to answer the question you asked.

I must disagree with your implication that the fact of terminal illness contradicts the truth that God is all-powerful. The broader context of your question has to do with the wisdom of God and is part of the larger reason why God allows people, particularly those who trust in Him, to die.

The question of death is inextricably bound up in the fact of human sinfulness. People die because they sin. Hence, as sinners we are all terminally ill. Before there was sin in the world, there was no death. Sin enslaves and kills every sinner. Disease is but one of the many manifestations of sin in our world. Other manifestations are war, hatred, dishonesty, pornography, etc.

This is not to say that people who are obviously terminally ill are worse sinners than those who presently do not appear to be terminally ill. It is not proper or Biblical (with certain exceptions) to suggest that an illness is the direct result of a certain sin. Those who suffer terrible pain are not necessarily terrible sinners (see John 9:1-3). However, they cannot claim to be without sin.

Christians follow Jesus' directive and example when praying for anyone in pain. They do not order God to remove the pain. They submit their requests and themselves to God as Jesus did with the words:

But let it not be as I want it, but as You want it (Matt. 26:39).

Look at that passage in the Bible, and you will read what terrible distress Jesus was experiencing when He spoke those words.

As a servant of the Good News of Jesus Christ, I have ministered to those who were dying. Dying people who *lived* by faith in Jesus *died* trusting in Him. They knew their bodies were getting weaker, but their spirits did not fail them, because the Spirit of God testified with their spirits that they were and are the children of God (Rom. 8:16). In good times they gave glory to the God who was with them. In bad times they were not about to curse Him who was still with them. Since they knew that Jesus had taken away their sins, they knew that God would not forsake them in death. They demonstrated the truth of Scripture that

Precious to the Lord is the death of those He loves (Ps. 116:15).

Those who remain after the death of a loved one who died in the Lord weep because they have suffered a loss. They do not cry for the dead loved one, because they know that person is blessed and rests from his or her labor and suffers no more (see Rev. 14:13). Their weeping will be turned into eternal joy on Resurrection Morning. We who are in Christ have this comfort even though we are terminally ill.

The Lutheran Hymnal has a prayer for a happy death. Pray this modified version with me: "Confirm, we ask You, Almighty God, Your unworthy servants in Your grace that in the hour of death the adversary, the devil, may not prevail against us but that we may remain faithful unto everlasting life through Jesus Christ, Your Son, our Lord. Amen."

And, God, What About Using DRUGS AND ALCOHOL?

What is the difference between drink and drugs for pleasure and for escape? Thanks!

From our study of the Bible, we can say that God makes a clear distinction between the use (for pleasure) of alcoholic beverages and the abuse (for escape) of alcoholic beverages. However, God disapproves of the use of drugs except in medical treatment. We have summarized our answer to your questions in the following chart:

	Pleasure	Escape
Alcohol	Yes	No
Drugs	No	No

Concerning drink: God is not a killjoy. Do you remember the very first miracle that Jesus performed? It was to change water into wine at a wedding reception (John 2:1-11). From this we conclude that Jesus approves of the pleasure of drinking wine. In fact, the psalmist praises

God for "making grass grow for the cattle, and plants for man to cultivate to get food from the ground: wine to cheer up a man . . ." (Ps. 104:14-15a).

Using wine or other drink "to get out of one's head," for pure escapism, however, is condemned by the Bible as drunkenness. The sin of drunkenness puts one outside the kingdom of God (see Gal. 5:19-21). Drinking for pleasure, when done to excess, is drunkenness. The same Bible which speaks of wine cheering up a man also warns against the abuse of wine. Prov. 20:1 is a stern warning:

> Wine makes people scoff, and liquor makes them noisy; anyone who staggers with it isn't wise.

In Prov. 23 we read:

> Don't keep company with those who drink too much wine or eat too much meat for pleasure, because a drunkard and a glutton will get poor, and being in a stupor will dress you in rags (verses 20-21).

Later, in the same chapter we read:

> Who has woes? Who has misery? Who has quarrels and who is groaning? Who gets wounded without a reason? Whose eyesight is blurred? Those who linger over their wine; those who keep coming to taste mixed wine. Don't look at wine when it is red, when it sparkles in the cup and goes down smoothly. Finally it bites like a snake and stings like an adder. Your eyes will see strange sights, and your mind will say confused things (verses 29-33).

It is when you "linger over" your drink that you become drunk, and the things described in the Proverbs passages do happen. Using drinking as escape will surely lead you into the drunkenness that is destructive of real trust in the Lord Jesus. Booze becomes lord in the life of the boozer, and that is a sin against the First Commandment, which reads:

Do not have any other gods besides Me (Ex. 20:3).

Concerning drugs: The use of mind-affecting drugs is fooling around with *pharmakeia,* which is listed with drunkenness in Galatians. *Pharmakeia* is the word in the original Greek text of Gal. 5:20. It is translated "witchcraft" in the King James Version and "sorcery" in the Revised Standard Version. We regard the RSV's "sorcery" as the better translation, since it represents the simplest meaning of *pharmakeia,* which is "drugging." Taking mind-affecting drugs is not something new; it was not invented by modern society. The practice of drugging oneself and/or others was very common in pre-Christian times. Such drugging was done for pleasure, for escape, and frequently in association with the worship of pagan gods. The practice of drugging is condemned by God in His Word to us.

The early church heard and heeded the Word it received from the apostle Paul in Ephesians:

> Don't get drunk on wine, which means wild living. But let the Spirit fill you as you speak psalms, hymns, and songs to one another . . . (Eph. 5:18-19a).

The church at the end of the 20th century needs to hear and to heed the same Word. (See also the following question about getting DRUNK.)

And, God, What About Getting DRUNK?

I was wondering if drinking—getting drunk—is a sin. (I know it is, but I'm hoping it isn't). Having a very hard time quitting it. I don't know for sure if it is a sin, but I have a feeling it is. If the answer is no this is great, but if it is yes please give me some help to beat it. Please give me yes or no answer. Thank you.

Yes, drunkenness is a sin. It is a work of the flesh rather than a fruit of the Spirit. St. Paul tells us:

> Now, you know the works of the flesh. They are: sexual sin, uncleanness, wild living, worshiping of idols, witchcraft, hate, wrangling, jealousy, anger, selfishness, quarreling, divisions, envy, drunkenness, carousing, and the like. I warn you, as I did before, those who do such things will have no share in God's kingdom (Gal. 5:19-21).

All these "works of the flesh" are self-destructive or abusive to part of God's world. It is very apparent to medical doctors, to family and friends of "drinkers," to members of Alcoholics Anonymous (AA) and AA-related groups, as well as to law enforcement people who deal with DWI (Driving While Intoxicated) "accidents," that drunkenness is self-destructive.

Have you noticed in your reading that when the word "drinking" is used you understand it to mean the consumption of alcoholic beverages and it does not sound so bad. However, when the word "drunken" is used it takes on a negative meaning. How often have you used the term "drinking" to mean "drunken," just so it didn't sound so bad?

In the original Greek of the New Testament there is a clear distinction between drinking and drunken. The verb "to drink" is *pino*, while the verb "to get drunk" is *methuo*.

The word *pino* is never used in a negative way in the New Testament. *Pino* is the common word for ingesting a liquid. It is the word used in connection with Jesus' institution of the Lord's Supper. Jesus gave His disciples a cup of wine and told them to drink (*pino*) it. He said what He was giving them was His blood shed for the remission of their sins. *Pino* is also used figuratively for experiencing something and would coordinate with our use of "drinking something in."

Methuo means "to get drunk" or "to become intoxicated." It appears in several forms in the New Testament and is never used in a positive way. It means not so much the use of wine but the *abuse* of wine. The problem does not reside in the wine (beer, whiskey, etc.); the problem resides in the abuser of alcoholic beverages.

In your question you state ". . . but if it is yes, please give me some help to beat it." We assume from this that you drink more than you should and therefore are an abuser of alcohol, not just a user.

The first step in the process is to admit that you have a problem. You have done this by asking the above question. Now you need to ask God to forgive you and then to give you the strength not to abuse alcohol. You need to ask for His help each day and also to stay away from those places that have contributed to your drinking problem. You need to be filled with the Spirit of God, not spirits, for we read:

> Don't get drunk on wine, which means wild living. But let the Spirit fill you as you speak psalms, hymns, and songs to one another, and with your hearts sing and play music to the Lord, always thanking God the Father for everything in the name of our Lord Jesus Christ (Eph. 5:18-20).

The only real alternative to drunkenness, and for that matter any sin, is the forgiveness and the life with God that is offered all people in Jesus Christ. The Spirit of God has the power to convict you of sin, and He also has the power to turn you to Jesus and in Him to transform your life. Please help yourself to the help that God offers you. He offers that help in Jesus. He offers that help through His holy Word, the Bible, and He offers that help through those who are already filled with *the* Spirit.

It is our prayer that your efforts to control your abuse of alcohol will succeed. Sometimes, however, the temptation to abuse alcohol is so strong that you cannot control yourself. We would suggest that you talk to your minister, who can counsel you and/or refer you to groups in your community who can help you.

One group that has a good record of helping people who need help helping themselves is Alcoholics Anonymous (AA). AA can be found by looking in your local phone book under AA or Alcoholics Anonymous. Your local Mental Health Clinic is another good source of information and help. (See also the previous question about using DRUGS AND ALCOHOL.)

And, God, What About Controlling EMOTIONS?

How can I come to control my emotions, instead of them controlling me?

Emotions are powerful, and it is clear that they can be captured by the sin in us. Emotions that have been enslaved by sin need to be delivered from sin as much as every other part of us.

Be assured that Jesus delivers us from all sins and all corrupted emotions. When we believe and confess Jesus as Savior, He also becomes our Lord. When we submit ourselves to the lordship of Jesus, we find that His love controls us. If we let Him, He will even control our emotions. With Him in charge of our lives, we can be certain that our emotions will be under control.

Unfortunately, nothing in us is perfect this side of heaven. Therefore we constantly keep Jesus from exercising perfect control of our emotions or lives. We Christians always live under the grace of God and attempt to walk by faith and not by sight. Walking by faith includes submitting ourselves, our emotions and our requests, to God in prayer.

Dear Lord, I know that my emotions are sometimes controlled by the sin in me. Please give me the strength to overcome sin's control and submit myself to Your control, through Jesus Christ. Amen.

And, God, What About the FIRST CHURCH?

Can you give me Biblical proof concerning the "first" church? My dad oftentimes will tell me that the Catholic Church is the "first."

The New Testament Greek word for "church" is *ekklesia*. It is found 115 times in the New Testament. In 112 places the word is rendered "church" in the King James Version of the Bible. In only three places is it translated as "assembly." This translation is justified since the crowd referred to was not a group of Christians drawn together around the Word of God (see Acts 19:32, 39, 41).

In the Gospels we find that Jesus used the word "church" only three times. In Matt. 16:18 He spoke of building His church upon the rock. In Matt. 18:17, in the steps of admonition, He spoke of the offended party speaking to the "church." In that same verse He also said that if the unrepentent sinner refuses to listen to the admonition of the "church," then that person is to be regarded as an unbeliever and outsider.

Most of the 115 New Testament uses of the word "church" are found in the writings of the apostle Paul. Luke, in the earliest history of the church (the Acts of the Apostles), does use the word 22 times. John also uses it 22 times in his Third Epistle and in Revelation. The author of the Epistle to the Hebrews uses the word twice, and James in his epistle uses it only once.

The word *ekklesia* is also found in the Greek version of the Old Testament. There it is sometimes used to refer to the Jewish congregation of Old Testament believers.

Based on the above, it is possible to say that the "first" church was made up of those true believers in the Old Testament who first looked forward to the promised Messiah. In my opinion those first true believers were Adam and Eve. They heard and believed the promise of God that He would send the Seed of the Woman to crush the seed of the serpent (see Gen. 3:15). They mistakenly thought their first child was that Promised One (see Gen. 4:1). From our first parents the promise concerning the Deliverer from sin and death was passed from one generation to another. So it is possible to think of the first human couple as the "first" church.

After the birth of the Promised Deliverer, one can suggest that the "first" church consisted of the 12 apostles Jesus gathered to Himself (see Mark 3:13-19). He "called them out" from the world to follow and serve Him. "Called out" is the literal translation of *ekklesia*.

It was during their three years of "seminary training" that Jesus asked His seminarians: "Who do people say the Son of Man is?" (Matt. 16:13). In that question Jesus was asking what people in general thought of Him. They gave several answers. He then asked them the more personal question: "Who do *you* say I am?" (Matt. 16:15). Speaking for himself and the group, Simon Peter said: "You are the promised Christ . . . the Son of the living God!" (Matt. 16:16). After telling Peter that the Father in heaven had revealed that truth to him, Jesus said that He would build His church (*ekklesia*) on this rock, and the forces of hell would not overpower it (Matt. 16:18).

Because the name Peter means "rock," the Roman Catholic Church has claimed that this is the basis for saying that Jesus built His church on Peter. Many Christians do not accept that interpretation. We hold that in Matt. 16:18 Jesus was indicating that He would build His church on the conviction of faith that Peter expressed. To us this means that the church will be found wherever people confess what Peter confessed in that passage.

Elsewhere in the New Testament the church is said to be "built on the foundation of the apostles and prophets," with Jesus Christ as the Cornerstone (Eph. 2:20). Thus, all who trust in Jesus and adhere to the teachings of the apostles are members of the "first" church.

Another place you can look to find a description of the "first" church is in Acts 2. There you find that Jesus fulfilled His promise to send His followers another Counselor. The Holy Spirit came upon the believers, and they witnessed for Jesus.

In his Pentecost sermon the apostle Peter accused his hearers of crucifying the Messiah of God. The people were crushed by his accusation. They asked the apostles how they could be absolved of their guilt. Peter told them: "Repent and be baptized, every one of you . . ." (Acts 2:38). Many of them did just that, so that on the Day of Pentecost 3,000 people were added to the followers of Jesus. We are told that in subsequent days the Lord added even more people to the nascent church (Acts 2:41, 47).

Those who were added continued together in the apostles' doctrine, in fellowship, in breaking of bread, and in prayer (see Acts 2:42). The Acts of the Apostles traces the very early history of the church. It is only toward the end of that book that reference is made to Rome. The "first" church was not in Rome and was not the Roman Catholic Church. It was in Jerusalem, and amazingly was comprised of Jewish Christians, the first "Jews for Jesus."

Did you know that the believers in Christ were first called Christians in Antioch, Syria? You can find that account in Acts 11:26. Antioch, Syria, actually became the launching pad for the missionary effort that brought Christianity to Rome. As a result, it is also possible to designate the congregation at Antioch as a "first" church.

Where was the first church? It all depends on what "first" you are looking for. (See also the question on CATHOLIC.)

And, God, What About Laying a FLEECE Before You?

I've heard reference to the Bible passages where it is mentioned that a follower of God in the Old Testament was unsure of God's will on a subject and laid a fleece on the ground and asked that God show him His will by either covering the fleece with dew or letting it remain dry. Is it proper to test God in this way by "laying a fleece" before the Lord (i.e., if You want me to do this, cause such and such to happen)?

A The idea of "laying a fleece before the Lord" originates with a historical incident recorded for our learning in Judg. 6:36-40. The judge Gideon is the one who "tests" God in that account.

When you study the Bible, you must be careful to distinguish between what is descriptive and what is prescriptive. What is descriptive is recorded for our information, but not necessarily for our emulation. What is prescriptive would include either an explicit or implied instruction for us to follow. Hence, everything recorded in the Bible is not there for us to emulate. For instance, the Bible tells us that King David committed adultery and murder. Obviously, we are not to follow David's example in these activities. These negative activities are recorded in the Bible for our learning.

The authors believe that Gideon's "laying a fleece before the Lord" is in the descriptive category and is a negative example recorded for our learning. Other people, however, feel it is in the prescriptive category. They think it is written for us to follow in seeking the will of the Lord. In the remainder of this answer, we will try to show our reasons for feeling the fleece incident is descriptive.

Most activities which are prescriptive are reported in more than one place in the Bible. We do not read anywhere else in the Bible that we should follow this example of Gideon's behavior. Gideon is mentioned in Heb. 11 (the Heroes of Faith chapter), but he is not a hero because of this incident.

Frankly, Gideon does not seem at his best in the concluding verses of Judg. 6. God complied with Gideon's wishes, but that does not mean that He was pleased with Gideon's requests. You will note that in the text Gideon was not satisfied with the Lord's first compliance; he required a second proof. We think that one revelation or directive from the Lord on a particular subject should be enough for an obedient servant of the Lord. We do not think, therefore, that Judg. 6:36-40 is given to us as an example to follow.

We also see the incident of Gideon and the fleece as descriptive because we are aware of the many places in the Bible where the Lord tells us not to "tempt" or "test" Him. When Jesus was tempted by the devil, one of His responses was:

"It is also written," Jesus answered him, "Don't test the Lord your God" (Matt. 4:7).

Jesus was quoting Deut. 6:16. He did that in response to the devil's challenge that He throw Himself down from the pinnacle of the temple. The devil even had the audacity to quote the Word of God (Ps. 91:11-12) as justification for Jesus to tempt or test God. In 1 Cor. 10:9 the apostle Paul urges us not to tempt Christ the way some 23,000 people did in the

49

wilderness. So the idea of giving God a test in which He must confirm His Word and will to us doesn't fit very well into the understanding that we are to be His obedient sons and daughters.

The above answer does not mean that an obedient servant of God will always know God's will. There are times in the Christian's life when he/she does not know or is not sure what God would have him/her do. Fortunately, unlike Gideon who had only a few books of God's Word (perhaps the first six books of the Old Testament), we have 66 books of God's Word. In the books of the Bible we have the will of God revealed to us. Therein He reveals to us both His law and His Gospel. In the law He reveals to us what is pleasing in His sight, while in the Gospel He reveals to us that there is forgiveness with Him for all sinners in Jesus. If we want to do what is pleasing in the sight of God, we will first search His Word to see what it says about our concern. When we do, we will learn that in order for some activity to qualify as God-pleasing it must be done from the context of faith (trust) in Jesus, according to the guideline of the Ten Commandments, to the glory of God, and for the benefit of our fellow human beings. In all things let us pray with Jesus:

> But let it not be as I want it but as You want it (Mark 14:36b).

(See also the question on Proper PRAYERS.)

And, God, What About Worrying About FOOD?

What is meant by not worrying about food? I'm try to lose weight. Does it mean to eat and not worry about it or to diet and not worry about eating? Which one? Please explain.

It seems to us that you are thinking of Jesus' words:

> So I tell you, don't worry about what you'll eat or drink to keep alive or what you'll wear on your bodies. Isn't life more than food, and the body more than clothes? (Matt. 6:25).

Jesus continues:

> Don't worry, then, and say, "What are we going to eat?" . . . or, "What are we going to wear?" The people of the world run after all these things. Your Father in heaven knows you need them

all. Strive above all to live under God's rule and according to His righteousness, and you'll get all these other things too. So, don't worry about tomorrow. Tomorrow will take care of itself. Each day has enough troubles of its own. (Matt. 6:31-34).

In these words Jesus urges us to make the spiritual the priority of our lives. He urges us not to think only about material things. He says that when we seek *first* the kingdom of God, all the material things we need will be provided for us.

We cannot quote words of Jesus and the Bible about losing weight. However, St. Paul writes that we should do all things in moderation (Phil. 4:5 KJV). Moderation in eating would seem, for most people, to be the answer to overweight and overeating problems.

If, however, you have a major weight problem, we urge you to talk to a medical doctor for advice on your condition. Then follow the doctor's advice as best you can, asking God in prayer to help you in this task.

And, God, What About FORGIVENESS?

I drink, smoke pot, yet maintain very good grades with a good outlook on life. Will God forgive?

Will God forgive drinking? This is not a sin.
Will God forgive getting drunk? Yes, but . . .
Will God forgive smoking pot? Yes, but . . .
Will God forgive very good grades? This is not a sin.
Will God forgive a good outlook on life? This is not a sin.

Yes, God will forgive getting drunk and smoking pot, *but* you can only enjoy His forgiveness when you are truly sorry for your sins.

Yes, God will forgive you because: "You forgive us to have us fear You" (Ps. 130:4) and, "You, Lord, are kind and forgiving, full of love for all who call to You" (Ps. 86:5). God offers this forgiveness to all sinners. God "wants all people to be saved and to come to know the truth" (1 Tim. 2:4).

That is why He sent His only Son Jesus "to lift up from us," "to lift away from us," "to deliver us from," and "to liberate us from" our sins. Enclosed in the quotes are the literal definitions of some of the original words for "to forgive" which are used in the Bible. Jesus lifted our sins from us and took them to the cross with Him, and there He suffered the eternal consequences of all our sins. In fact, it has been well said that on the cross Jesus suffered hell—complete separation from God—for all people for all sins for all time.

Forgiveness is what God offers to every one of us. Since God's forgiveness has been paid for by Jesus and is offered to us free of charge, it is really an offer we cannot afford to refuse.

But at the outset we wrote, "Yes, but . . ." Yes, God will forgive, but you can enjoy His forgiveness only when you are truly repentant.

John, the apostle of love, wrote:

If we say we don't have any sin, we deceive ourselves, and the truth isn't in us. If we confess our sins, we can depend on Him to do what is right—He will forgive our sins and wash away every wrong (1 John 1:8-9).

And David, the psalmist, wrote:

How blessed you are if your wrongs are forgiven and your sins covered. How blessed you are if the Lord doesn't count you as guilty, and if there is no deception in your spirit. When I kept silent, I wore out my limbs groaning all day long. Day and night Your hand lay heavy on me; I was turned to ruin by the summer heat. I told You my sin and didn't cover my wrong. I said, "I will confess, O Most High, I will confess my wrongs, O Lord." And You took away my sin and guilt (Ps. 32:1-5).

The wicked suffer much! But if you trust the Lord, He will surround you with love (Ps. 32:10).

As you have read above, you can see that we need to acknowledge our sins and confess them to the Lord.

We need to change our mind about sin; only then can we really *enjoy* His full and free forgiveness. God, via the Holy Spirit, is willing and able to do that for you and in you.

And, God, What About Differing GIFTS?

Why is it that God allows some people (Christians) to do little studying and yet get good grades, while others really work hard and only get "C"?

Remember when you played on a seesaw? Your friend sat on the ground end of the board and you tried to push your side down so you

could get on. When you pushed on the board near the center (fulcrum), you could not lift your friend off the ground. Then another person, about the same size as you were, came to your end of the seesaw and with little or no effort lifted the first friend in the air. Why? The second friend pushed down on the very end of the board and used the principle of the lever to multiply his or her effort. Relating this to your question, would you say it was unfair that you worked hard and didn't move your friend while the second friend did little work and lifted the seesaw rider? Of course not. Have you seen the poster which reads, "Work Smarter, Not Harder"?

When it comes to making good grades, the person who has a difficult time may not be studying correctly. Not doing well on an exam may indicate that you are not studying the right information. You may have learned the names of the generals in a war while the instructor may have wanted the dates of the battles. Your teachers usually give some indication as to how important they consider certain people, places, dates, and events. If you have difficulty picking out the teacher's main emphasis, it is certainly proper to ask the teacher if you should stress names or dates in your study. It is also a good idea to talk to your fellow students about what they think the teacher is empha- sizing. You must do your own learning, but you can also work with other people to get on the right track.

If you continue to have trouble with exams, there are many counselors and books that can teach you study skills. There is no reason to feel bad about asking for help in learning how to study.

One additional admonition. Do not equate time with hard work. There are many variables which can influence the correlation of the apparent effort and time with the apparent end result. If your best effort is a C, then that is an acceptable grade. If, however, your grade is a C and you did not use your full talents, then this C is an unacceptable grade.

God has made us all, but He has not made us alike. This difference was immediately evident when God created the first two people. "He created them male and female" (Gen. 1:27). The first children born were also different. "Abel grew up to be the shepherd of a flock, but Cain became a man who worked the ground" (Gen. 4:2). In the New Testament Christ told about the three servants who were given money ". . . each according to his ability" (Matt. 25:15). From this we can see that God likes variety and wants us to be different. God also tells us that we are equal in His sight. This does not mean that we are all the same. The concept of equality before God and man has to do with equal worth, not equal ability. Every human is a unique individual from the moment of conception, but God has called us all to share equally in His kingdom. Thus, God has given us equal righteousness in Christ, not equal ability in this world.

This concept of equal before God, but unique, applies to all humans.

Just because you are a Christian does not change the basic facts of humanness.

Permit an example from the world of sports that can be applied to your real concern about apparently unequal rewards from hard work. In the 1979 Super Bowl, quarterbacks Terry Bradshaw and Roger Staubach, both publicly acknowledged Christians, worked hard before and during the game. It was a close game (35-31), and both played well; yet, one was a winner and one was a loser. Since they are both Christians, was that fair? Yes, since in football we expect winners and losers. The authors, who watched the game, suggest they were both winners, since their conduct on the field and off (particularly after the game) was exemplary by the standards of Christian behavior.

The same parallel can be drawn from the Biblical examples given above. We are certain that Cain and Abel both worked hard in their jobs as farmer and shepherd. Yes, "The Lord looked kindly at Abel and his offering, but He didn't look kindly at Cain and his offering" (Gen. 4:4b-5a). Is this fair since both worked hard? Yes, since God told Cain: "Sin is crouching at your door and wants to get you" (Gen. 4:7). Here God was judging their hearts, not their hard work.

In the Matthew account of the servants, we see that the person with $10,000 and the person with $4,000 worked with the money given them. When each was asked to give an accounting of his trust, each returned the original amount with a substantial increase. Their reward was the same:

> You proved you could be trusted with a little. I will put you in charge of something big. Come and be happy with your master (Matt. 25:21, 23).

The person given $2,000 buried it in the ground. When he was asked for an accounting, he returned to the master the original $2,000. His reward was: "Throw this good-for-nothing slave out into the dark where there will be crying and grinding of teeth" (Matt. 25:30). Again, God was judging the servants' motives.

So, do the best with the equipment you now have. Make every effort to learn how to improve your use of that equipment. Don't overlook any opportunity to learn. Don't be ashamed to admit you need help. Remember, God has called us to be faithful stewards of His many gifts. He Himself is the One who gives the increase. He blesses the labors of our hands.

And, God, What About the GIRL Back Home?

Pastor:
My girl back home is giving me a lot of trouble. She says that she wants to have some fun and see if she really loves me. She

hangs around bars and lounges, and I don't like that.

We have gone together for two years, but during the last six months we have had arguments. Our backgrounds are very different. I am ambitious and she is not. I have accomplished many things in high school and college. She complains about what she calls my $25 college talk. When I try to explain things in a meaningful way, she accuses me of using **logic.**

I was raised in a Christian home, whereas her parents have provided a rather ill-mannered environment for her and her brothers and sisters to grow up in. I have tried to meet and talk with her parents, but they will not meet or talk to me. I don't respect her parents.

I am frustrated and confused. I love her, but I don't know why. How can I cope with breaking up with her? I think she wants to "have some fun" and then get back together again later. I don't like that idea.

I guess I just have to get this off my chest. I appreciate it that you are willing to "listen." Please give an answer soon. Don't worry, I won't do anything stupid. I think too much of myself and family to do that. I guess I've just got to stop looking back and begin looking to the future.

Thank you for any help you may care to give me.

A Friend, I am happy to be an "ear." Permit me to play back to you what I "hear" you saying. I do so in a format which should show you the vivid contrasts you have cited in your relationship with this girl.

You are here.	She is there.
You are in college.	She apparently is not.
You don't go for hanging around bars.	She thinks hanging around bars is the thing to do.
You say you love her.	She says that she has to have some fun to see if she really loves you.
You were raised in a Christian home.	She was raised in a . . .
You do not respect her parents.	She . . . ?

You respect your parents.	She . . . ?
You have tried to meet and talk with her parents.	Her parents will not meet or talk with you.
You use language which has become part of your way of life and expression because you are a college student.	She does not understand and apparently does not care for what she calls your $25 college talk or your logic.

You seem aware of how different your backgrounds are. It would seem that the difference in your backgrounds, your attitudes, your education, your religions, your accomplishments, and your goals are much greater than the things you have in common. Think about the prospects for the future with such a person. Could you change enough to fit her pattern of thinking? I doubt it. Can you expect her to change enough to fit your pattern of thinking? Again, I doubt it.

You say you love this girl but you don't know why. Frankly, with all the contrasts that you cited, I don't know why either. You must use your head in matters of the heart.

Don't rely only on your feelings and marry the girl in the hope that she will change. The same advice goes for the girl.

In addition, do not think that if you were to marry you could live your married life apart from your families. Despite the fact that many people deny it, when you marry someone you become a member of his/her family. I would not think that prospect is very appealing to you.

Friend, I think you have answered your own questions. Learn from your past experiences. Don't keep looking back. Look to the future. I think you are going to have to accept the idea that your relationship with this girl "has had it."

To say such a thing and to emotionally accept it is not easy. The confusion you feel is similar to the grief one suffers when a loved one dies. There is a feeling of loss that defies description. But grief is something people get over. They soon realize they will not be able to replace the person who is gone. They learn to substitute activities with other people, particularly those who have had the same experience. Do not think that your experience is unique.

In conclusion, I must say that as a Christian I am convinced from the Word of God and from personal experience that one who trusts in Jesus as Savior and serves Him as Lord should not become seriously involved or marry someone who does not believe in Jesus. God says to us in His Word:

Don't be yoked with unbelievers. How can right and wrong be

partners? Or how can light have anything to do with darkness? How can Christ agree with the devil? Or what does a believer have in common with an unbeliever? (2 Cor. 6:14-15).

And, God, What About Long HAIR?

 This may sound weird, but I read once that it is a sin to have long hair. Is this true?

Deut. 22:5 may be the passage that someone has applied to hair, although it doesn't make explicit reference to it. This passage reads:

> A woman shouldn't wear a man's things, and a man shouldn't wear a woman's clothes, because the Lord your God is disgusted with anyone who does these things.

We can imagine that this passage may have been applied to the length of hair. We believe that this passage means that men ought to look like men and women ought to look like women. It is, however, very doubtful that Moses, the human author of the passage quoted above, had a crewcut. The length of hair among males and the relative length between male and female is a rather faddish thing.

Another passage that comes to mind is in 1 Cor., where the apostle Paul discusses the God-ordained relationship between men and women, husbands and wives. In that context he writes:

> Doesn't nature itself teach you it's disgraceful for a man to have long hair but that it's a woman's glory to wear her hair long? (1 Cor. 11:14-15a).

Perhaps this is the passage you recalled. If it is, you must be careful in the way you use this passage. Again, it's very doubtful that Paul had a crewcut. His hair may have been as long or longer than the hair on the heads of some women today. It is also reasonable to assume that few women in Paul's day cut their hair. Hence, it would be safe to relate the meaning of Paul's statement to the one from Moses and point out that a man ought not to wear his hair in such a way that he gives the appearance of being a woman, or vice versa.

Despite the allegations that the Bible, and St. Paul in particular, are "sexist," we hold that it is only in Christ that you, whether male or female, can grow up into the full stature of what God intended you to be. It is by the grace of God alone that we become children of God. As children of God, both male and female, we can equally have eternal life and look forward to a glorious inheritance in heaven. That is wonderful! For this we praise the Lord.

NOTE: Hair is mentioned many times in the Bible. Some of the passages are 2 Sam. 14:11b, 26; Job 4:15; Matt. 5:36; 10:30; John 11:2; 1 Tim. 2:9; 1 Peter 3:3.

And, God, HELP Me!

Somebody please help me.

Somebody does want to help you. That somebody is anybody who is in Christ. He or she will comfort you with the comfort wherewith God has comforted him or her. If you want someone who is in Christ to help you, you will have to talk with a Christian about the specific things that are troubling you.

Jesus Christ can help you directly. He searches for the lost. Like a shepherd, He searches until he finds the one lost sheep out of the hundred that are safe. He would have none be lost. He would be your Refuge and Strength, your Help in every trouble. May we introduce you, a helpless and lost sheep, to the Good Shepherd?

When you have accepted Christ, you will appreciate the prayer of St. Paul for the believers at Ephesus when he wrote:

> May God the Father and the Lord Jesus Christ give our fellow Christians *peace* and love with faith! His love be with all who have an undying love for our Lord Jesus Christ (Eph. 6:23-24).

This is also our prayer for you.

And, God, What About Getting HUNG UP on You?

I'm on probationary status, and will get kicked out of school for good if I don't make the grades. I'm afraid to "give in to God" because I'm afraid I'll get hung up on Him and spend comparatively little time on studies. Help!

If you are not doing well in your studies, then you really have little to lose if you commit yourself and throw your cares upon the Lord.

He invites us, every one of us, with all our cares and woes, to come to Him. He promises peace, and He tells us why: He cares for us. Then with His peace we can face the problems of life with the full force of our God-given minds.

I don't think you have to worry about getting "hung up on God." Surely you realize that there are many intelligent people whose studies did not suffer because of their commitment to Christ. Even secularists recognized that Martin Luther, who surely was a man of God, was a genius. Isaac Newton was both an early scientist and a man of God. There are many of our contemporaries whose commitment to God does not detract from their intelligence. I would hardly think such people can be characterized as "hung up on God."

The problem with which you are struggling is really a matter of priorities. The Christian is one who follows the directive Jesus has given us to "Strive *above all* to live under God's rule and according to His righteousness" and who then has the assurance that "You'll get all these other things too" (Matt. 6:33).

And, God, Why So Little About JESUS' Youth?

 Why is there so little written or known (to my knowledge) about Jesus Christ between the time He was a child up until the time of His early 30s?

You are correct when you write that there is little written about Jesus from the time of His infancy until He was 30 years of age. Exactly *why* we do not know; so I am unable to give a simple answer to this question. However, permit a few comments that can contribute to understanding the long lapse in the Gospel accounts of Jesus' life.

First, as one who trusts in Jesus and in His Word, I assume that God did not feel it was necessary for my salvation that I know much about Jesus' life during the unreported period. That makes sense to me because I am well aware that not everything Jesus said and did, even during His three-year ministry, is reported to me in the Gospels. "His disciples saw Jesus do many other miracles that are not written in this book" (John 20:30). But I am confident that what has been written in the Bible has been written so that I might "... believe Jesus is the promised Savior, God's Son, and by believing have life in His name" (John 20:31).

Of course, you realize that the Bible was not written only for me; it was written also for you. The purpose for which it was written is the same for both of us.

Second, the gospels possess eyewitness and earwitness authority concerning the events and the sayings they report. Two of the gospels (John and Matthew) were written by apostles, who accompanied Jesus during the days of His ministry. The other two (Luke and Mark) were written by men who were closely associated with apostles. Hence, most of what is reported in the gospels took place before the very eyes of the writers. Those writers did not follow Jesus prior to the beginning of His public ministry, at about age 30. Thus, the few things reported from the time of His birth, as well as His appearance at the temple in Jerusalem at age 12, are considered to have been told by the Virgin Mary, who was still alive during her Son's days of public ministry.

St. Paul wrote that the purpose of "... the Holy Scriptures ... [is] to make you wise and save you through faith in Christ Jesus" (2 Tim. 3:15). He further said:

> All Scripture is inspired by God and is useful for teaching, showing what is wrong, improving and training in right living, so that a man of God is ready and equipped for every good work (2 Tim. 3:16-17).

We conclude, then, that what is in the Bible can do the job God wants done. We do not need any further information about Jesus to be made wise unto salvation.

And, God, What About JUDAS?

Q *I have always wondered if Judas was offered any free will in betraying Christ; and if so, wouldn't it have ruined a predetermined plan if he hadn't betrayed Him? I guess I just don't understand how free will and a predetermined plan can both occur at the same time. I think there is a single word that covers what I mean by "predetermined plan" but I can't think of it.*

A Thank you for giving me the opportunity to answer a question that is perplexing to many people. We have problems when we try to fit together the statement: "God definitely planned and intended to have Him betrayed" (Acts 2:23a) and the concept that Judas had a free will.

This answer is based on the conviction that we humans cannot possibly understand everything about God or His counsels. However, the answer is also based on the conviction that what God has revealed to us in His holy Word, the Bible, does provide all that is needed for our salvation.

In dealing with Judas, one must go to the gospels to see what happened and what Jesus Himself said about His betrayer. You will find such information in Matt. 26:21-25, in Mark 14:18-21, and in Luke 22:21-23. In Matthew's gospel and Mark's gospel you will find exactly the same wording when Jesus said:

The Son of Man is going away as it is written about Him, but woe to that man who betrays the Son of Man! It would be better for that man if he had never been born (Matt. 26:24 and Mark 14:21).

In Luke's gospel we read that Jesus also said:

The Son of Man is going as it is decreed, but woe to that man who is betraying Him (Luke 22:22).

What had been determined was that the Son of Man, the Messiah, would be betrayed into the hands of evil men, who would crucify Him (Acts 2:23). That was God's plan for Jesus and for our salvation. Jesus would be the Lamb of God, who would take away the sins of the world. There was no mistake made in crucifying Jesus. It was not an accident of history that Jesus died on a cross or that a friend betrayed Him. God planned it that way, and God knew beforehand that that is what would happen.

In fact, God revealed in the Old Testament that somebody close to the Messiah would turn Him over to His enemies. John 13:18 tells us:

But what the Bible says has to come true: He who eats My bread kicks Me.

Jesus seems to be referring to Ps. 41:9, which reads:

Even My friend whom I trusted, who ate My food, gives Me a hard kick.

Besides this passage about betrayal of the Messiah by a close associate, there are numerous other Old Testament passages which refer to the suffering and death of the Savior. Most notable among these is Is. 53, which reads in part:

He was despised, forsaken by men,
a man of sorrows who knew suffering.
People covered their faces so as not to see Him.
He was despised,
and we thought nothing of Him.
But surely He has taken on Himself our sickness

and carried our sorrows. . . .
Yet the Lord planned to crush Him
and slay Him (Is. 53:3-4a; 10a)

That Jesus' suffering and death were part of God's plan of salvation from sin for all people does not excuse any of those who participated in putting Him to death. In his famous Pentecost sermon the apostle Peter accused all his hearers of crucifying Jesus (Acts 2:36). All sinners are responsible for Jesus' suffering and death, since He suffered and died in our stead. Jesus took our sins, our guilt before God, and our punishment upon Himself. In exchange He gave us His righteousness.

Now, back to Judas. Even though God had planned in advance that His Son would be betrayed and put to death on the cross, this does not excuse Judas for actually perpetrating that heinous deed. One cannot excuse Judas for his betrayal of Jesus any more than one can exonerate him for any of his other sins. While it is true that someone would betray Jesus, Judas did not have to be the one. Judas did not have to betray Jesus. Jesus' words to Judas at the table during the Last Supper are understood by many students of the Bible to be a last plea and warning to Judas about what he was about to do. Even in the Garden of Gethsemane it almost seems that Jesus is pleading with Judas by calling him "Friend" (Matt. 26:50).

After Jesus was condemned to death, Judas was full of remorse. However, he did not turn to God in repentance, nor did he accept the forgiveness Jesus offered. He rejected it at the moment when Jesus was suffering and dying to procure it for him. That is truly sad, since God's grace is free and universal. Peter also betrayed Jesus. He also was full of remorse. However, he did turn to God in repentance, and he did accept the forgiveness Jesus offered. (Compare Matt. 27:1-10 with Matt. 26:69-75 and John 21:15-19.)

It is true that Satan entered the heart of Judas (Luke 22:3), but Judas did not have to let him in. Judas did not have to make arrangements with Jesus' enemies for His betrayal. Neither Judas, nor any other sinner, can use the cop-out: "The devil made me do it." That did not work in the Garden of Eden, and it has never worked since then. We human beings are responsible to God for our conduct. We cannot blame somebody else, or circumstances, or even God Himself. As Jesus pronounced woe over Judas and many other sinners in the gospels, so He pronounces woe over all sinners. However, Jesus, the Redeemer, pleads with all sinners to see that they fall short of the glory of God, to repent, and to accept the remission of sins He offers. Repentance and remission are not cop-outs; they are the way God has planned that we can enjoy the eternal blessings of the Good News.

Simply put, it was God's plan that Jesus be betrayed, but Judas did not have to do it. Judas was responsible for what he did. Judas could have had forgiveness even for his terrible deed, just as Peter received forgiveness. He could have had forgiveness, just as any other sinner can still have forgiveness.

And, God, How Can I KNOW You?

 Hi! I know a girl who believes in everything except God (Jesus, etc.) and all the teachings. She says she doesn't because she doesn't "know" and that there's **no definite proof** *of God and Jesus. What do you think?*

 I would assume that your friend believes that there was a George Washington; yet unless she is older than our nation itself, she did not come to know him by a face-to-face meeting. Your friend "knows" George Washington solely on the basis of the witness/ testimony of others. Yes, she may read some papers that President Washington wrote, but even then she is accepting the opinion of someone else that what she is reading is authentic.

A Christian accepts the testimony and the witness of others that Jesus was born, lived, died, and rose again as reported to us in the Holy Bible. To do such a thing is as rational as accepting the fact that there was a man who was born, lived, and died called George Washington. The writers of the gospels claim eyewitness authority for the things about which they write.

But, your friend may say, George Washington lived only 200 years ago while Jesus lived 2,000 years ago. Yes, this is true; yet the earliest manuscripts of the complete New Testament available today were copied within 250 to 300 years after Jesus. Manuscripts of parts of the New Testament are available that were written even closer to Jesus' time.

If your friend can accept the eyewitness reports about George Washington which have come to us from 200 years ago, then she should be able to accept the eyewitness reports about Jesus which are only 200 years removed from Jesus Himself.

However, do not ask her to take our word for it. Invite her to read and discuss the Bible with you. Share your faith in Jesus with your friend.

Hark the voice of Jesus crying,
"Who will go and work today?
Fields are white and harvests waiting;
Who will bear the sheaves away?"
Loud and long the Master calleth,
Rich reward He offers thee;
Who will answer, gladly saying,
"Here am I, send me, send me"?

Let none hear you idly saying,
"There is nothing I can do,"
While the souls of men are dying
And the Master calls for you.
Take the tasks He gives you gladly,
Let His work your pleasure be;
Answer quickly when He calleth,
"Here am I, send me, send me!"

The Lutheran Hymnal, 496:1, 4

With the help of the Holy Spirit you can talk to your friend.

And, God, What About Being LONELY?

 Pastor, I know Jesus is there, but I still feel lonely, as though there were a void inside me. I'm lonely, insecure, and afraid. At times I feel and act childish, not really wanting to grow up.

A I'm sorry you feel so bad. I hope it makes a difference to you that a fellow member of the body of Christ feels at least some of the hurt you feel. Your fellow Christians know that it is part of their responsibility as well as part of their privilege to share and bear your burdens with you. You are not alone. Jesus and the friends of Jesus would like to help you. Please help yourself to the help God offers.

God helps you through the means of grace which He has given to His church here on earth. Take advantage of the means of grace, which are the Word of God and the sacraments (Baptism and Holy Communion). It is via these means of grace that God brings us to true trust in Jesus. It is also via these means of grace that He sustains us in the faith.

In order to enjoy the means of grace, you will need to read the Word of God. After reading the Word of God, you will want to share with others what you have learned. Therefore it is important to involve yourself in the work and fellowship of Christians. Join the youth groups and Bible study classes offered at your church. Attend worship services and partake of the Lord's Supper. The Word of God and the sacraments will fill the void in you. By joining with fellow Christians you will not have time to be lonely, insecure, and afraid.

Are you looking for love when you act childish? When you become involved with other Christians, you will grow in Christ and in His love. Motivated by that love, you will put away childish things (see 1 Cor. 13:11) and grow up.

And, God, What About True LOVE?

Today the word "love" is used quite freely, and I was wondering how a guy can tell if he loves a girl and vice versa. I know that we should love one another like brother and sister, but I mean something that is deeper than that; I mean the type of love that could lead to marriage.

I would agree with you that the word "love" is used very freely these days. It is used so freely that it has lost much of its original meaning. Today the word "love" is being used to mean anything from a first-meeting infatuation to a casual sexual encounter. God's definition of love does *not* include such uses of the word.

The love that leads to marriage usually begins with a mutual attraction. This is the start of a growth process that continues for life. The initial attraction may be any number of things. I remember being attracted to my wife by her smile, a smile that showed her teeth even though she was wearing braces. I figured anyone who would smile under those circumstances must be worth knowing. I'm not certain what attracted her to me, but it was a mutual attraction. A good, long-term relationship must also recognize the other person as an individual who possesses the inestimable worth of a unique human being.

Along with respect for the other person's individual worth, there must be an appreciation of what that other person has done and is capable of doing. With such respect and appreciation, the two people can begin to work together as a team. Anything less than teamwork before and during marriage is "bad news." The guy and the gal who are usually competing with each other will not make good marriage partners.

Since God Himself chose to compare the relationship between Christ and His church to that of a husband and wife, it would seem that in this relationship one can find the deepest possible love. In the relationship between Christ and His church, we are told that He, Jesus, loved the church so much that He gave Himself for her. Jesus loved us so much that He sacrificed His life for us. Hence, if you love someone else so much that you are willing to give yourself for her or him, then such love would be the optimum kind of love. (See Eph. 5:21-33.) Such love is certainly not lust, for it is unselfish and self-giving. Such love is also not a mere emotion or sentiment. Such love involves a real and abiding commitment. Look at 1 Cor. 13:4-8a. There you can read:

Love is patient. Love is kind. Love isn't jealous. It doesn't brag or get conceited. It isn't indecent. It isn't selfish. It doesn't get angry. It doesn't plan to hurt anyone. It doesn't delight in evil but is happy with the truth. It bears everything, believes everything, hopes for everything. Love never dies.

Much of what masquerades as "love" today obviously does not qualify according to these words of God.

In conclusion, permit me to suggest that you rethink your statement that the love between siblings is not as deep as that between husband and wife. The respect, the unselfish commitment, the service we render to other members of our family can be as deep as that between husband and wife. It is true that one *expresses* love toward one's parents and one's siblings differently than one does toward one's spouse. However, that difference of *expression,* which is God-ordained, does not mean that the love is not as deep. You might also think about the time when you will have children of your own. You will love them. Such love will not be shallow; it will be deep.

And, God, What About MARRIAGE Ceremonies?

How is it that a man and woman were joined as husband and wife before the ceremony of marriage became a custom? I'm sure it hasn't always been the way we know it today.

Marriage customs have not always been as they are today. There is a great deal of variety in marriage/wedding customs around the world. Customs even vary from one section of our country to another. Some of the variations in customs are, of course, related to ethnic and religious differences.

It appears that the earliest records, both Biblical and extra-Biblical, indicate that there has always been some kind of ceremony in which a man and a woman were joined together as husband and wife.

In the opening chapters of the Bible there are implications of a marriage rite. In Gen. 1, immediately after God created man and woman in His own image, it is reported:

And God *blessed* them. "Have children," God told them, "and multiply and fill the earth and control it . . ." (Gen. 1:28a).

In Gen. 2 we read that God said:

It isn't good for the man to be alone. I will make him a helper such as he needs (Gen. 2:18).

After the Lord God made the first woman from the first man and *brought* her to the man, the man *said:*

Now this is bone from my bones . . . and flesh from my flesh. She will be called woman because she was taken from man (Gen. 2:23).

And then it is stated that henceforth:

A man leaves his father and his mother and lives with his wife, and they become one flesh (Gen. 2:24).

What we are told about the marriage ceremonies of the patriarchs in the Old Testament is rather sketchy. When we read the accounts in the Book of Genesis, we sense that some sort of ceremony was used, but we are not given any details. In Gen. 24 Rebekah's parents expressed their conviction that it was the Lord's will that their daughter should leave them and become the wife of Isaac, Abraham's son. Her send-off with Abraham's servant was done with considerable care, and interestingly, with her consent. In Gen. 29 all the men in the place were gathered and a feast was held when Jacob was given Laban's daughter for his wife.

After the Jews returned from the Babylonian captivity, a marriage contract was signed by the couple; perhaps even the families signed it. A meal was part of the celebration. Cups of wine, as a toast and a blessing, were offered. The bride wore a white dress, a veil, and was bedecked with jewels and garlands. There was music, singing, and dancing.

Marriage ceremonies changed and developed in many and varied ways throughout Old Testament times. By the time of the New Testament, the following customs were observed. There were two separate ceremonies, the betrothal and the wedding. Hebrew Christian scholar Alfred Edhersheim, in his classic work *The Life and Times of Jesus the Messiah,* reports that in the betrothal the couple pledged themselves to each other. They were blessed with the Word of God and prayer. Although they were considered husband and wife from the time of betrothal, they did not live together or have sexual intercourse until after the wedding. The longest period of time between the two events seems to have been one year.

Early extra-Biblical records also indicate that there was some sort of marriage ceremony.

The *Ras Shamra* texts from ancient Ugarit, which was on the northern section of the Syrian coast, include something about wedding customs among the people of that culture. The material is thought to have come to us from approximately 1400 B.C., which is about the time of Moses. In what is called "The Legend of King Keret" there are the following relevant lines.

The blind man gave his *benediction.**
The bridegroom produced the *bride-price,*
Burning to claim his wife,

Yea, to acquire his beloved.
As locusts which occupy the fields,
As hoppers the desert marches,
They went a day, a second [day];
After that, at sunset on the third [day],
They reached the *shrine* of Atherat of Deposits,
Even [the shrine of] the *Goddess* of Oracles;
There Keret of Th' made a vow . . . [emphasis added].
(D. W. Thomas, ed., *Documents from Old Testament Times,* New
York: Harper and Row, 1958, p. 119.)

    *Our meaning is established by Arabic cognates. The blind
man, incapable of active service, can at least speak an auspicious word, which had the effect, it was thought, of influencing
Providence by auto-suggestion . . . (Ibid., p. 122).

The Stele of Hammurabi (c. 1792—1750 B.C.) does not report a
marriage ceremony as such but is filled with a great deal about proper
and improper conduct with regard to those who are married and those
who are not married. The paragraphs of the Code of Hammurabi imply
that there was a public event by which people knew who was married
and who was not.

Hence, the earliest records available to us indicate that there has
always been some sort of ceremony in which man and woman were
joined together as husband and wife.

In the United States today we seem to have three forms of marriage
ceremonies. We have the traditional marriage in church. We have a
civil ceremony in a court or other public place. We also have the
nonmarriage marriage in which a man and a woman agree to live
together without the benefit of one of the "legal" ceremonies. However,
because of the potential legal problems, formal written contracts have
been drawn by some partners. The partners claim they are not married,
but what is the contract but another form of marriage ceremony?

From the above we can see that the cohabitation of man and woman
has always been taken as a serious commitment. As such, society has
always legitimatized marriage with public statements and ceremonies.

Christians recognize that marriage is from God. Therefore it is to be
entered into with all seriousness, ever mindful of our obligation to each
other and to God (see Eph. 5:21-33).

And, God, What About METAPHYSICS and Religion?

*Can you please explain to me the relationship of metaphysics
to the religion you preach? I am looking for a clearer
understanding of both metaphysics and religion!*

A Metaphysics can be defined as the "system of principles underlying a particular study or subject." Religion can be defined as "a cause, principle, or system of beliefs held to with ardor and faith" (*Webster's Seventh New Collegiate Dictionary*). In this chapel the Christian religion and a Christian metaphysics are preached. The principles of our religion are all found in the Bible. We believe that the Bible is the inspired Word of God and as such is the *only* sufficient source of information about God.

The Bible tells us all we need to know about our relationship with God and with other humans. In the beginning God and humans were in perfect harmony. But then Adam and Eve disobeyed God (sinned) and broke that perfect relationship. Even today all people have a broken relationship with God, since we all disobey God's law as found in the Bible. This is the bad news for us, since we humans cannot do anything to repair the broken relationship with God.

The Good News, or Gospel, on the other hand, is found in the message of Jesus Christ. Jesus repaired our broken relationship with God when He died on the cross. God accepted His sacrifice as full payment for all of our breaking of His laws. When we accept Jesus Christ, we are returned to a perfect relationship with God.

With these basic principles from the Bible, the Christian can answer philosophical questions such as:

Who am I?
Where did I come from?
Where am I going?
Why?
What is right and what is wrong?
For what should I live?

This book contains a number of metaphysical questions and answers. We would encourage you to read and study the writings of authors like C. S. Lewis and Francis A. Schaeffer. They write about the relationship between metaphysics and Christianity in very exciting ways. Of course, we would also expect you to read the basic textbook of Christian metaphysics and the Christian religion, the Bible.

And, God, What About MOSES Killing the Egyptian?

In Exodus where Moses killed an Egyptian for striking one o his fellow people, why didn't God reprimand Moses for th act? Do you think Moses went to heaven?

A I am convinced Moses went to heaven. My conviction is based on the fact that Moses is listed as a man of faith in Heb. 11. In Heb. 11:24-28 Moses is said to have acted by faith. The expression "by faith" occurs three times in that section. Amazingly it even says:

> He [Moses] chose to be mistreated along with the people of God rather than to enjoy the pleasures of sin for a short time. He regarded disgrace for the sake of Christ as of greater value than the treasures of Egypt, because he was looking ahead to his reward (Heb. 11:25-26 NIV).

The mistreatment Moses suffered was thus considered to have been for the Christ, who is Jesus. Moses, then, believed in the Messiah to come. Therefore, when we read in Deut. 32:48-52 that the Lord God told Moses to ascend Mount Nebo to die, we can be certain that while no man knows where his body lies, God does (see Deut. 34:6). God took Moses, His servant, to be with Him in heaven. Also, when our Lord Jesus was transfigured, Moses appeared with Elijah and talked with Jesus (Mark 9:4). This indicates that Moses was alive with the Lord.

Your question about Moses killing the Egyptian slavedriver (Ex. 2:11-15) is, however, not as easy to answer. You are correct, as far as I know, that there is no recorded reprimand of Moses by God for that killing. There are at least two possible explanations for this.

The first explanation is to consider the slaying of the Egyptian to have been justified. In this way Moses is not considered a murderer, because he acted out of righteous indignation to save his fellow Hebrew. To suggest this is to put Moses' action in the category of the justified "police" action. Moses then was acting in defense of a defenseless citizen. Hence, Moses did not need a reprimand, nor did he need to repent, because he was executing God's wrath on the evildoer (see Rom. 13:4 KJV).

This first explanation is not quite satisfactory to the answerer because there is no indication in the Bible that Moses possessed the authority of a government as defined in Rom. 13:1-7. In Ex. 2:11-15 Moses seems to be taking the law into his own hands. Such a vigilante action falls under the warning of Rom. 12:19, which reads:

> Don't take revenge, dear friends, but let God punish, because the
> ⸃le says: I alone have the right to avenge. I will pay back,
> ⸃e Lord.

would have had to repent and seek the forgiveness of the Egyptian. I believe, since Moses is considered a he did seek and receive the forgiveness of the Lord.

The second explanation is more satisfactory to this answerer.

There is forgiveness and life even for murderers. This forgiveness is clearly shown in the way Jesus from the cross promised paradise to the penitent thief, who undoubtedly was also a murderer (Luke 23:39-43). That, however, does not mean that the individual who takes the life of (murders) another may not have to pay with his or her own life (see Gen. 9:6). There are temporal (earthly) consequences for our sinful actions. Moses suffered those consequences. His own countrymen feared him, and he had to flee for his life (See Ex. 2:14-15). Nevertheless, the early consequences of sin do not cancel the eternal benefit of the forgiveness one can enjoy in Jesus. Jesus gives eternal life. You, too, are offered this forgiveness and life with Christ. That offer is too good to refuse.

And, God, What About Being MYSELF?

What is wrong with being myself if it doesn't hurt other people?

Being yourself is fine. People should be free to enjoy what is to their liking and to develop their own God-given talents and potential. Such "being yourself" ordinarily does not hurt other people.

Being yourself is not, however, an absolute personal freedom. Our freedom is restricted by the laws of our society, which are designed to protect the rights of other people. We are also responsible to God for all our acts, whether in public or in private. Nothing is hidden from His eye.

But God is not the great super-snooper or Big Brother in the sky. God does not spy on us to see what we are doing wrong. God is the shepherd who looks after the sheep. The shepherd's task is to keep harm away from the sheep and also to keep the sheep from harming themselves.

God is motivated by love for us. Therefore His basic laws are designed to help us live a life that is pleasing to Him, not harmful to ourselves or others. Hence, some of the Ten Commandments tell us what to do and others tell us what not to do.

It is because God has such high regard for all His creatures, especially humans, that He does not want us to harm ourselves. He does not want us to become self-centered or narcissistic. He does want us to be ourselves, but He also wants us to be involved with other people. In

fact, shortly after the beginning of time it was God who said:

> It isn't good for the man to be alone. I will make him a helper such as he needs (Gen. 2:18).

People can do their own thing as a child of God or as a child of the world. It is our prayer that you do your own thing as a child of God.

Only when you know that you have been bought with a price will you want to do what is pleasing to God. When you know that Jesus redeemed you with His precious blood, you will not insist that you have the absolute freedom to do whatever you please. Are you such a person?

And, God, What About Belonging to NON-CHRISTIAN ORGANIZATIONS?

 Hello! I was just wondering what God thinks about non-Christian organizations? For example: the kind that stress unity with the members. And what does He think about the rituals and ceremonies one goes through to join?

 It is good to hear that you are concerned about not wanting to compromise your Christian convictions. More people need to be as perceptive about this issue as you seem to be.

I am convinced that God does not want His people joining organizations in which they would compromise their commitment to Him and to His Word. It is clear that the Lord did not want Israel to be intimately involved with her heathen neighbors. When she did get so involved, the Lord said that Israel, His "wife," had been unfaithful, and He called her to repentance. It is also clear that God does not want Christians, the New Israel, involved with the surrounding heathen people so that they lose their peculiar nature (see 1 Peter 2:9 KJV). He does not want a follower of Jesus to be "yoked together" (KJV) or "mismated" (RSV) with unbelievers (2 Cor. 6:14). Through the apostle Paul, God tells us to mark those who cause divisions and offenses contrary to what we have learned (in the Bible) and avoid them (Rom. 16:17 KJV).

Hence, the Christian must be concerned about an organization's purposes and principles. Those organizations that hold principles and advocate teachings that are contrary to what the Bible teaches are those which the Christian cannot support, much less join.

The person who is committed to Jesus will not take part in rituals and ceremonies addressed to Greek gods or goddesses, Hindu deities (as in the Transcendental Meditation ritual), or any modern form of nature worship. To do such things is either a subtle or not-so-subtle denial that Jesus is the One and Only Way to God.

The Lutheran Church—Missouri Synod has taken a strong stand against such compromises of the "holy, Christian, and apostolic" faith. In its *Handbook* (1975 edition) all its congregations, pastors, and teachers agree that:

> The Synod has declared itself firmly opposed to all societies, lodges, and organizations of an unchristian or antichristian character (14:01, a).
>
> Pastors and laymen alike must avoid membership or participation in any organization that in its objectives, ceremonies, or practices is inimical to the Gospel of Jesus Christ or the faith and life of the Christian church (14:03, a).
>
> It is the solemn, sacred, and God-given duty of every pastor properly to instruct his people concerning the sinfulness of all organizations that—1. explicitly or implicitly deny the Holy Trinity, the deity of Christ, or the vicarious atonement; 2. promise spiritual light apart from that revealed in the Holy Scripture; 3. attach spiritual or eternal rewards to the works or virtues of men; and/or 4. embrace ideologies or principles that clearly violate an express teaching of the Holy Scriptures concerning the relationships of men to one another (14:03, b).

Permit an example from personal experience. I was once invited to join an honorary society on a college campus. I asked the leader of the organization if there was a required initiation ceremony. He said that there was one. I then indicated that I would not be willing to participate in any ritual or subscribe to any oath without knowing its content beforehand. I was promised, but never given, a copy of the ritual. As a result I did not join the organization.

In this world there are organizations that are not Christian but at the same time are not antichristian. It is possible that a Christian might belong to such an organization and work for its goals without compromising his or her trust in Jesus. Such organizations would be those which have been established to serve various human needs. Government, for example, is called an institution of God (see Rom. 13:1-7). Therefore a Christian can certainly be involved in government and/or politics. Such involvement is to be an expression of commitment to Christ. The Christian is not involved to conform to the world but to transform the world (see Rom. 12:2).

And, God, What About Heaven for NON-CHRISTIANS?

What about our non-Christian friends when they die? I've lived in a Buddhist country for two years and have many Buddhist friends. They also believe in heaven and hell. I

cannot accept the idea that they will go to hell if they aren't Christians.

A Christians believe and confess with the apostle Peter:

No one else can save us, because in all the world there is only one name [that of Jesus] given us by which we must be saved (Acts 4:12).

Peter's confession of faith is based on statements of Jesus like:

I am the Way, the Truth, and the Life. . . . No one comes to the Father except by Me (John 14:6).

And:

If you have seen Me, you have seen the Father (John 14:9b).

And:

Anyone who believes in the Son has everlasting life. But anyone who will not listen to the Son will not see life, but God's wrath rests on him (John 3:36).

The uniqueness of the revelation of God in Jesus of Nazareth as well as the all-sufficiency of the work of salvation He has accomplished on our behalf are the reasons why Biblical Christianity teaches that it is necessary that every human being be taught about Jesus and His love. It was necessary that Jesus reveal the invisible God to us because we cannot by our own efforts make ourselves right with God. Humans cannot free themselves from the snare of sin. When we have been liberated from sin, knowing that all our sins are forgiven and that we possess the gift of eternal life, then we want others to know the same blessings we enjoy. We know that God has not been good to us because we are good but because He is good. That goodness has been revealed to us in Jesus. That goodness becomes ours when we put our trust in Jesus as our only Savior.

Now to your question about Buddhists in particular and non-Christians in general. First, let us review what Buddhism teaches about death, heaven, hell, and salvation. I am certain you will see that there is a great deal of difference between Buddhism and Christianity on these very crucial issues.

Siddhartha Gautama, who became the Buddha, or the Enlightened One, did not preach gods. He preached a way of life. He did not claim to be God or God incarnate.

In evaluating the human condition, Gautama concluded that *suffering* is man's basic problem. He insisted that suffering is the root of all human troubles. In his teaching he stressed what are called the Four Noble Truths. Those four truths are:

1. The recognition that suffering is man's basic problem,
2. That the cause of suffering is the false craving for the alluring things of this world,
3. That a person must search for a way to overcome such false craving, and
4. That the search can be successful only by following the Eightfold Path.

The Eightfold Path to Enlightenment proposed by Buddha has to do with right thinking and conduct. Buddhism teaches that when one follows the teachings of the Buddha, then one will become enlightened. Such a person will achieve *nirvana*, which has been described as the state of emptiness, the end of self, the ceasing of the cycle of reincarnation. *Nirvana* is achieved by the person himself. The Buddhist does not pray to God or to gods for enlightenment. In fact, in his last instructions the Buddha said in part:

So, Ananda, you must be your own lamps, be your own refuges. Take refuge in nothing outside yourselves. . . . Do not look for refuge to anything besides yourselves (Merle Severy, ed., *Great Religions of the World*, National Geographic Society Book Service, Washington, D.C., 1971, p. 164).

As a result of such teaching Buddhism has been called atheistic. Buddhism denies the existence of a Creator who stands outside of man and judges the actions of human beings. Instead Buddhism teaches the impersonal law of *karma. Nirvana*, not heaven, is the ideal goal of the Buddhist. A reincarnation lower then one now endures, not hell, is the bane of the Buddhist. As the way of salvation, the Buddhist must depend solely upon himself. Since there is no concept of sin in Buddhism, the Buddhist feels no need for the forgiveness of sin or a Savior from sin.

Note that neither God nor gods are mentioned in Buddhism's Ten Commandments:

1. Thou shalt not kill any living being.
2. Thou shalt not take what is not thine.
3. Thou shalt not commit adultery.
4. Thou shalt not prevaricate, but shalt speak the word of truth.
5. Thou shalt not partake of any intoxicating liquors.
6. Thou shalt not partake of food after midday.

7. Thou shalt not be present at any dramatic, dancing, or musical performance.
8. Thou shalt not use any personal adornment or perfume.
9. Thou shalt not sleep on a broad, comfortable bed.
10. Thou shalt not be the owner of any gold or silver.

(Max Stilson, *Leading Religions of the World,* Grand Rapids: Zondervan Publishing House, 1964, pp. 27—28.)

Buddhism differs from one location to another. It has assimilated local customs and other religions. There are two basic divisions within Buddhism—the southern and northern branches.

The southern Branch, called Theravada Buddhism, is found in Thailand, Cambodia, Laos, Burma, and Sri Lanka. It is the more conservative form of Buddhism. It offers salvation or enlightenment to very few people. Because of the limited offer of enlightenment its detractors call Theravada Buddhism *Hinayana,* which means the Lesser Vehicle. Theravada Buddhism regards the relics of the Buddha as well as the many images of the Buddha to be powerful. It has come to regard Buddha as a god. Salvation is merited; it is even possible to purchase a god's favor.

In opposition to Theravada Buddhism there is *Mahayana,* the Greater Vehicle, Buddhism. It offers enlightenment to more people and is the more liberal form of Buddhism.

The Buddhist is not taught that he is a sinner. He is not taught that he needs to repent of the sins with which he has offended the personal God of the Bible. He is taught, instead, that he must achieve enlightenment or salvation by his own efforts. If and when he does that, he will have escaped the cycle of rebirth and will cease to exist.

Buddha did not and Buddhism does not teach the same thing as the Christ and Christianity. He or she who accepts Jesus as his or her personal Savior from real moral guilt feels very sad that so many people in our world, including Buddhists, do not know the real joy of the full and free forgiveness that is ours in Jesus. The Christian feels the obligation to share the truths of God revealed in the Bible. That feeling of obligation compels the Christian to do personal mission work among those close to him or her and to support missionary endeavors which are dedicated to preaching the Good News of Jesus and His love to every creature. It is necessary that mission work be done, because without Jesus people are lost. Nobody can save himself or herself. Everybody in the world needs to know Jesus.

(See also the questions on WITNESSING as the Work of the Holy Spirit and Good WORKS.)

And, God, What About PERFECTIONISM?

 My brother (a Christian) says that once you become a Christian you can no longer sin, and sinning is very unnatural to the Christian. Yet, I still sin. Could you expand on this if possible?

 I respectfully disagree with your brother and the notion that after a person trusts in Jesus, he or she does not sin. I do not find any form of perfectionism in the Bible. This side of heaven, I do not expect to be perfect, nor do I expect to meet anyone who is perfect.

I base my conviction on the following:

> If we say we don't have any sin, we deceive ourselves, and the truth isn't in us. If we confess our sins, we can depend on Him to do what is right—He will forgive our sins and wash away every wrong. If we say we haven't sinned, we make Him a liar, and His word is not in us (1 John 1:8-10).

These words, which are the Word of God, were written by a *Christian* to *Christians*. Further comment as to whether or not Christians sin does not seem necessary. Personally, I do not want to call God a liar, nor do I want to deceive myself. Rather, I want His Word and His truth to be in me. I want His forgiveness and cleansing.

The apostle Paul writes to his friends the Philippian Christians:

> I don't mean I have already reached this or am already at the goal, but I eagerly go after it to make it mine because Christ Jesus made me His own. Fellow Christians, I don't think I have it in my hands. But one thing I do; I forget what is behind, reach for what is ahead, and with my eyes on the mark I go after the heavenly prize to which God has called us in Christ Jesus (Phil. 3:12-14).

It is obvious that the apostle did not think he "had arrived" morally. It is obvious that he does not think he is perfect (that is, sinless). He looks forward to something better than he is. He knew that there was something better ahead for him. I think every Christian can identify with the apostle Paul. Every Christian can and should look forward to what God has in store for him or her in His presence forevermore.

Since I still have the "old man" in me, I know that *by nature* I am inclined only to evil (see Rom. 7:14-25). I need to drown that "old man" every day. I need to beat him down and keep him under the control of the law of God so that I can live as a new creature in Christ Jesus. It is natural for me to sin, but when I submit myself to Christ and learn obedience from Him, then I can overcome that natural man and live by faith in the Son of God. The struggle between the "old man" and the "new man" in me continues as long as I am in this world. I am always in need of Christ's deliverance. I am always in need of His forgiveness and strength. I am confident that Jesus will not forsake me. I live under the grace of God; I put my trust in Him. I do not rely on my righteousness, nor do I trust my own understanding. I trust in Jesus, and I don't talk about being perfect or not sinning anymore. You can do that too. Jesus will help you.

And, God, What About Pulling the PLUG?

 What about "pulling the plug" on a life-line support system? Are you taking one's life, or is it already gone?

Your question is one that is difficult to answer, particularly because of the many implications and ramifications involved. In the answer below we would offer six principles that should be taken into consideration before arriving at a God-pleasing decision.

First, we hold the position that each human life is of inestimable value and is invested with the highest dignity by God, the Creator of all life. This position is called the principle of the sanctity of life. We agree with Dr. Albert Schweitzer, who wrote:

> The fundamental principle of ethics, then, is reverence for life. All the goodness one displays toward a living organism is, at bottom, helping it to further preserve its existence. Humanitarianism consists in this principle, that a man is never to be sacrificed for an end.

Because of the high value of each human life, we must make a major effort to preserve that life.

Second, when we are dependent on a support system, that dependency does not take away our value or dignity as human beings. You are certainly aware that from conception until long after birth we were all completely dependent on our mothers. Hence, we do not feel that dependence on a "life-line" of support indicates that one has ceased to live.

Third, it is clear that with modern medical technology it is possible to keep a person alive far longer than in the past. It is now possible to keep some people alive that once were considered "impossible cases." We believe in the impossible. We believe that with God all things are possible. At times, however, we humans think we know all the answers.

Several years ago the "plug" was pulled on a young lady who was in the "impossible case" category. To the amazement of all, she lived for years after the "plug" was pulled.

Fourth, we need to consider the definition of "death." Just when is a human being dead? The Christian answer is when the soul has gone to heaven to be with Jesus forever.

Fifth, we believe with Job of old:

Naked came I from my mother's womb, And naked will I return. The Lord gave and the Lord took away—The Lord's name be praised (Job 1:21).

This text is commonly used at funerals. One who believes that God is "the Lord and Giver of life" (the Nicene Creed) is one who is willing to wait on that Lord in all things. We prefer to let God do the "taking away" of a life, as we do not wish to assume God's role.

Finally, in all circumstances we need to seek God's guidance in prayer and through pastoral counsel. God invites us to call upon Him in the day of trouble. He promises to be our Refuge and Strength as we strive to make decisions. He promises to hear our prayer and provide us with an answer.

And, God, What About PRAYERS for Me?

Pastor, do you know who I am? I have given Jesus charge of my life. Please pray for me. I have so little faith, so little trust. I want someone to hold me, to love me. Do you want to know who I am, besides the chief of all sinners? Please pray for me. Thank you.

I am, of course, pleased that you are ready to cast your cares and yourself on Jesus. He is the only Savior. He is our only Help in every need. Remember, He did it all for you. Do not depend on yourself. Depend on Him; He will never fail you.

I will pray for you. I will pray that you will grow in your trust in Jesus.

Do you know that many people pray for you each and every day? If you have Christian parents and/or sponsors, they were charged at your baptism with the responsibility of praying for you. Many churches pray for fellow Christians. The Lutheran Church in its General Prayer, which is a part of its regular order of service, prays:

> Be Thou the Protector and Defender of Thy people in all times of tribulation and danger; and may we, in communion with Thy church and in brotherly unity with all our fellow Christians, fight the good fight of faith and in the end receive the salvation of our souls (*The Lutheran Hymnal*, p. 13).

So you see, prayers are said for you by your name as a human and your family name of Christian.

You must, of course, also pray for yourself. One prayer that Jesus taught us to pray is:

> Father, may Your name be kept holy, Your kingdom come, Your will be done on earth as it is in heaven. Give us every day our daily bread. Forgive us our sins, as we, too, forgive everyone who sins against us. And don't bring us into temptation (Luke 11:2d-4).

Prayer is a talk with God. Talk with God in your own words. Tell Him what is of concern to you. Ask Him to forgive your sins. Ask Him to show you His way. God will answer, because He has assured us:

> So I tell you: Ask and it will be given to you. Search and you will find. Knock and the door will be opened for you. Anyone who asks receives; anyone who searches finds; and anyone who knocks, the door will be opened for him (Luke 11:9-10).

And, God, What About Proper PRAYERS?

Is it all right to pray for anything that is in line with the Lord, or just certain things? What can you pray for and what can't you pray for? Are there limits or anything as long as it isn't sin?

The Bible clearly reveals to us that God wants us to speak to Him, in prayer, about *anything* that is of concern to us. We should make our requests with boldness in matters such as the spiritual blessings of forgiveness, His Spirit, a stronger faith, deliverance from evil and temptation, the assurance of eternal life, a blessed death, etc. We can even submit our requests and ourselves to God concerning such matters without saying "if it is Your will." It is His will that we have and enjoy such blessings.

However, on those matters about which God has not revealed His will to us we must always add, as Jesus did in the Garden of Gethsemane, "If it be Your will" (Matt. 26:39). God has promised us "daily bread" (or necessities for this life), but He has not promised us "cake" (luxuries). On many matters of the body, rather than of the soul, God has not revealed exactly what His will for us is. Therefore we cannot assume that what we want is what He wants for us. Hence, on such matters we should always pray "according to Your good pleasure and gracious wisdom." When we pray we should never prescribe to God how and when He should do the thing for which we pray. We must always remember that when we pray we are submitting ourselves and our petitions to a King.

(See also the question on Laying a FLEECE Before You.)

A hymn based on Matt. 21:22 says:

What a Friend we have in Jesus,
All our sins and griefs to bear!
What a privilege to carry
Everything to God in prayer!
Oh, what peace we often forfeit,
Oh, what needless pain we bear,
All because we do not carry
Everything to God in prayer!

Have we trials and temptations?
Is there trouble anywhere?
We should never be discouraged—
Take it to the Lord in prayer.
Can we find a Friend so faithful
Who will all our sorrows share?
Jesus knows our every weakness—
Take it to the Lord in prayer.

Are we weak and heavy laden,
Cumbered with a load of care?
Precious Savior, still our Refuge—
Take it to the Lord in prayer.
Do thy friends despise, forsake thee?
Take it to the Lord in prayer;
In His arms He'll take and shield thee,
Thou wilt find a solace there.

The Lutheran Hymnal, 457:1-3

And, God, What About PRAYING to People in Heaven?

Since people here on earth ask others to pray for them in their daily lives like interceders for them to God, would it be right to pray or talk to the people already in heaven to intercede (pray) to God for them?

People of the world have tried to talk to the people of the past by praying to the saints, using a medium at a seance, worshiping their ancestors, etc.

The Christian, however, must follow the teachings of the Bible. The following shows God's answer to your question.

First, we read in Is. 63:16:

> You are our Father. Abraham doesn't know us, and Israel doesn't pay attention to us. But You, Lord, are our Father. Your name is "Our-Redeemer-from-Everlasting."

This clearly teaches that those who have died and gone to heaven cannot intercede or pray for us. Abraham and Israel were patriarchs in the Old Testament. They were the spiritual forebears of believers under the Old Covenant. They were with God when Isaiah spoke the words of this text, but notice it says that "Abraham doesn't know us," and "Israel doesn't pay attention to us." This means that they did not know what was happening on earth and thus were unable to do anything for Isaiah and his companions. What was true in Isaiah's day is still true today. Those who have died in the Lord and who are with the Lord do not know what is happening among us, and they are unable to do anything (including praying) for us.

Second, it is obvious from the above-quoted passage, as well as many others, that *God is our Help in every trouble* (see Ps. 46:1). It is in Him alone that we seek refuge. It is He who forgives all our sins, who heals all our diseases, who redeems our lives, and who crowns us with His mercy (Ps. 103:3-4 KJV and RSV). He is the only one in heaven who can help us.

Third, it is clear from passages like 1 Tim. 2:5: "There is one God, and One who brings God and men together, the Man Christ Jesus," that Jesus is the only Mediator between God and mankind. No one else takes Jesus' place, because He is the *only one* "who gave Himself as a ransom" for all (1 Tim. 2:6). Jesus paid the ransom by laying down His life for us. Jesus is the only Way to the Father. Jesus did it all for us. Thus, we always pray in Jesus' name, not in a saint's name.

Fourth, it is true that we are urged by God to pray or intercede for each other. We are even told to pray for our enemies and for those who despitefully use us (Matt. 5:44 KJV). Praying *for* someone else is not contrary to God's directive. But He directs us to speak *to* Him alone, *in* Jesus' name. Such intercessory prayer is urged only upon those who are still on this earth. There is no indication that there is a need for prayer in heaven. In heaven, in the presence of God, we shall have no needs. We will, therefore, not need to petition God for anything. We will only praise Him forever. In God's presence there will be fullness of joy and pleasures forevermore (Ps. 16:11 KJV and RSV). In Jesus, we have great expectations. In Jesus, the best is yet to come.

And, God, What About Proper PREACHING of the Word?

Do you believe there is an overabundance of preaching the Word of God? It almost seems as though people are being forced into religion. Example: people in the middle of campus passing out pamphlets and other things. This cannot be what God meant by preaching the Word.

I cannot comprehend there ever being too much proper preaching of the Word of God. Understand, however, that not all who call themselves Christians are true Christians. Certainly, the concept of "it doesn't matter which religion you follow as long as you are sincere" is false.

The Word of God is that which comes to us from God. The message of the Word of God has two parts. The Law part, which has the power to convict us of our sin, and the Gospel part, which shows us the power of Jesus Christ to forgive the sin.

Everyone needs to hear that message, because it is only by hearing it that one can come to faith in Jesus (Rom. 10:17). The apostle Paul even wrote that he was ready to be all things to all men, that by *all means* people might be won to Christ (1 Cor. 9:22 KJV and RSV). He thereby emphasized that the Christian needs to use every method currently available to get the wonderful Good News of Jesus and His love out to all people. I agree with the apostle Paul's emphasis on outreach.

We also read in the Bible that believers went *everywhere* proclaiming the Good News. They did that because they were commissioned to do so by Jesus (Matt. 28:19 and Acts 1:8). That Great Commission has not yet been fulfilled, since Jesus told us that when it is, the end of all things will come (Matt. 24:14).

Getting out the Good News is not solely the job of the professional preachers. The very first people to make known the birth of the Savior were humble shepherds. They simply told what they had seen and heard (Luke 2:17-18, 20). So, preaching the Word of God is not to be restricted to places like church buildings and chapels.

As mentioned earlier, everyone who *claims* to preach the true Word of God does not necessarily do so. The Mormons, for example, who are active worldwide, claim to preach the Word of God. However, upon close examination of that claim, one discovers that they do not teach the historical-Biblical Christian faith. They use Christian terms, but they do not define them in the same way that the Bible and the Christian church always have.

You seem concerned that people are being forced into religion. It appears that some forms of coercion are being used by certain cults. The proper presentation of the Gospel of Jesus Christ does not require the use of any form of coercion. The Gospel message uses the power of God's love for us fallen sinners. He loves us so much that He gave His own Son to die for us. He loves us and would have us turn from our sin and live in Him. Just as nobody can force you to love him or her, so God does not force us to respond to His love. We love Him when we are finally overwhelmed by how much He really cares for us.

It has been well said that

A man convinced against his will
Is of the same opinion still.

If God forced us to love Him, would it be a true love? Of course not. But when we accept Him, He gives us a new heart, a new spirit, and a new will. We can then say with St. Peter:

His is the glory and the power forever! Amen. (1 Peter 4:11c).

And, God, What About PSYCHOLOGY?

 Does psychology (the theories of the soul, mind, personality) have a place in religion?

 Your question is one that we are reluctant to write very much about, since neither of us has made psychology our field of study. Therefore we are not quite certain about the full ramification of many psychological terms.

The word "psychology" comes from a word that appears in the Bible. In the New Testament the Common Greek word *psyche* appears many times. It is translated as "soul," "life," and "self." It usually refers to a person's inner being. A man or woman's *psyche,* according to the Bible, is not to be identified with the body. The *psyche* is thought to be the real person, or one's personality.

Psychology, the study of the *psyche,* has a place in the life of the Christian. It should not, however, take the place of what God has revealed to us about ourselves. That there is a place for psychology in Christianity is demonstrated by Christian psychologists and psychiatrists who do not compromise their faith in Christ or deny Biblical teachings. They are able to use what humans involved in the study of the *psyche* have discovered to aid us in understanding ourselves.

If you have a personal problem, Christian ministers are trained to help you apply God's Word to solving the problem. For severe problems, the same ministers should be able to recommend a Christian psychiatrist and/or counselor.

And, God, What About READING the Bible?

 I would like to read the Bible. Can you tell me where to begin?

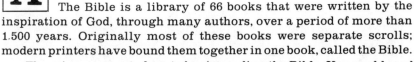 The Bible is a library of 66 books that were written by the inspiration of God, through many authors, over a period of more than 1.500 years. Originally most of these books were separate scrolls; modern printers have bound them together in one book, called the Bible.

There is no correct place to begin reading the Bible. You could read the books in any order, but such a way of reading the Bible does not provide the reader with an understanding of the relationships between the various books.

One reading plan would be to start with the first book, Genesis, and read through to the last book, Revelation. However, this procedure produces a number of problems for the new reader. One problem is that the order of the books in the English Bible is not precisely chronological. A second problem is the great amount of detail, e.g., family trees, found in many of the books. A third problem is that the books are various types of literature, including historical accounts, prophetic writing, and poetry.

A better reading plan, designed to minimize the difficulties for the new reader, would be to start with the gospels. The gospels report the life, the works, and the words of Jesus. The content of the books of the

Bible either flows to or from Jesus. In order to see how the whole Bible fits together you have to know Jesus and the life-that-is-more that He gives. We recommend that you start with Mark's gospel. It is fast-moving and short—you can read it in one sitting.

John's gospel is also a good book to start with, since it includes so many of the exciting things that Jesus has to say to us. After reading either Mark's or John's gospel, move on to the Acts of the Apostles. Acts is the earliest history of the Christian church. Next go to the "Beginning" and read the Book of Genesis. Read it with the realization that much of what is promised therein is fulfilled in Jesus the Christ.

As you read the Bible, remember that it reports things the way they really were. The imperfections of the men and women God chose to be His own are not glossed over. Every one of them was a sinner and needed forgiveness just as we do. That forgiveness is to be found in the sinless God-man who, the Bible reports, is the Center of all things. He is Jesus Christ.

And, God, What About Using RELIGION for Personal Gain?

Q *Do you believe that people are using religion for money-making purposes?*

A I am certain that there are people today who use religion to make money. But then, that is nothing new. In 2 Kings 5 you can read of a man by the name of Gehazi who did that very thing.

Gehazi's boss was the prophet Elisha. Without ostentation Elisha, as a servant of God, had healed Naaman, the Syrian army commander, of his leprosy. Naaman had wanted to lavish many gifts on Elisha, but the prophet would not accept them. However, after Naaman started for home, Gehazi ran after him and said that Elisha had changed his mind and would accept the Syrian's gifts. Actually, Elisha had not given such orders. Gehazi took the gifts and money for himself. When Elisha confronted Gehazi with this use of religion for personal gain, Gehazi lied. Elisha was not fooled, and Gehazi suffered for his sin. Read 2 Kings 5 to find out God's terrible, but fitting, punishment for this sin.

In Acts 8:9-24 you can also read about one Simon, a Samaritan sorcerer. He tried to buy the power of the Holy Spirit from the apostles. What is implied is that he wanted the power of the Spirit of God so that he could perform miracles and thereby make money and gain fame for himself. The apostle Peter pronounced Simon to be a wicked man and urged him to repent (which he did).

The fictional character Elmer Gantry would be an example of a man who used religion to exploit people. The fund-raising activities of some cults would be examples of the same type of behavior.

People have, down through the ages, used religion for personal gain, and undoubtedly they will continue to do so until Jesus comes again in glory. Christians do not worry about such things. Using the shield of faith, they keep their guard up against the abuse of religion.

When in doubt, Christians "test the spirits to see if they are from God" (1 John 4:1b). They do this by judging the teaching of the "spirits" against what the Bible teaches. In this way they follow the example of the early Christians in Berea, Greece, about whom Acts 17:11b says:

> They were very eager to get the Word and every day studied the Bible to see if those things [the teachings of Paul and Silas] were so.

And, God, What About Worrying About SALVATION?

 Since I am having troubles understanding things, would you help me? What if I ask God to forgive me all my sins through Jesus and asked Him to save me right this moment, but at the same time worried and wondered in my mind if He would really save me? Would He save me whether I worried or feared, or would He not save me because I didn't have enough faith to trust Him completely without worrying?

 Friend, stop worrying and trust what God tells you in His Word:

I will never leave you or desert you (Heb. 13:5c).

That is what God assures you and those who put their trust in Jesus as Savior and Lord.

Note that I did not say put *all* your trust, or *really* believe, or trust *completely* in Jesus. I did not use those adverbs because in every New Testament reference to trusting or believing in Jesus there are no adverbs; trust is trust is trust.

Understand that we are not saved because we believe. We are saved because of the grace of God in Christ. We are not saved by our faith; we are saved by the grace of God. It is through our faith that the grace of God comes to us and touches us. Now it is obvious that some people have broader and deeper faith than others. However, since it is what comes from God that delivers us from sin and death and brings us to eternal life, all who have faith get the same grace of God unto salvation.

My friend, God knows that even His children have fears, troubles, worries, and doubts. That is why over and over again in His Word He invites us to come unto Him, to call upon Him, and to cast our cares upon Him.

In this world, full of so many and varied troubles, Christians have many battles to fight. When we are in the middle of them, we can be certain that our relationship with God is dependent not on ourselves or our faith, but on God and His grace. The grace of God is inexhaustible, and He is unchangeable, so we can always rely on Him and His Word.

When you really feel down, pray with the man who said:

I do believe; help me with my unbelief (Mark 9:24).

Worry doesn't do a bit of good; in fact, quite often it does a great deal of harm. Most of all, don't worry about God. Not only can He take care of Himself, He can take care of you. Don't put your faith in faith; put your faith in Jesus. Jesus never fails. (See also the question on WORRYING.)

Jesus sinners doth receive;
Oh, may all this saying ponder
Who in sin's delusions live
And from God and heavens wander!
Here is hope for all who grieve—
Jesus sinners doth receive.

Oh, how blest it is to know:
Were as scarlet my transgression,
It shall be as white as snow
By Thy blood and bitter Passion;
For these words I now believe:
Jesus sinners doth receive.

Jesus sinners doth receive.
Also I have been forgiven;
And when I this earth must leave,
I shall find an open heaven.
Dying, still to Him I cleave—
Jesus sinners doth receive.

The Lutheran Hymnal, 324:1, 6, 8

And, God, What About the SANCTUARY Light?

 I'm a Roman Catholic—and I was always told (throughout my 12 years of Catholic education) that you can always tell if you are in a Catholic church by the red light (candle) burning in a lamp. This symbolizes the presence of God and distinguishes a Catholic church from some other denomination. I noticed when studying here one night that this church also has a red candle burning. What does it mean?

Since this is not a Roman Catholic church and since we do have a sanctuary lamp burning in the chancel of our chapel, then what you understood to be a distinctive symbol of a Catholic church is not. The red candle that burns in our Lutheran chapel also serves as a constant reminder of the presence of God. As Biblical Christians we believe that one of the attributes of God is omnipresence, i.e., the quality of being present in all places at the same time.

This chapel has been dedicated to the glory of the Triune God, with the Word of God and prayer. We believe that God comes to meet and bless us wherever His name has been recorded. God blesses us here with the Word of God and the sacraments of Holy Baptism and Holy Communion. It is well, then, that there be some reminder in our chapel that this is a place where God dwells and where He does great things for us. The seven candles by the far wall of the chapel are lit during each worship service as an additional reminder that God in Christ came and comes to dwell among us. During the services in which Holy Communion is celebrated, the two candles by the altar are also lit. These are to remind us that Jesus Christ is present with His true body and true blood when Communion is celebrated from our altar-Communion table. All burning candles remind us that Jesus is the Light of the world.

Not all Lutheran churches have sanctuary lights, so that does not distinguish us from others or identify us with one another. One of the principles used in Lutheran churches over the past 400 years is that symbols which do not detract from or add to Biblical teaching may be used in the church. As a result there have been and will be similarities between certain symbols in Lutheran churches and Roman Catholic churches, and Lutheran churches and Protestant churches. Whether there are similarities or differences in the symbols we use, it is our prayer that our ministry will give glory only to God and make people wise unto the salvation which is in Christ Jesus alone. Blessed be His holy and saving name!

And, God, SATAN Continues to Attack Me!

You have given me much spiritual balm. Please continue to pray for me, as Satan continues to attack me from every conceivable weakness. I'm scared of the future, but the Lord promised that He will never forsake me.

Indeed, the Lord knows those who are His own. He will not leave you or forsake you. He will be your Help in every need.

God is our Refuge and Strength, a very great help in time of trouble. We're not afraid even when the earth quakes, the mountains topple into the sea; even when its waters roar and foam, and the mountains shake in the middle of it (Ps. 46:1-3).

Until Jesus comes again we will be assailed by the wiles of the devil. He does not give up. He knows that his time is short, and that is why he is so active; he wants to "win" as many for his kingdom as he can. Below, you will find a few passages that are given to us by God in His holy Word as warnings to keep us alert to the wily ways of the devil.

You're not fighting against flesh and blood but against the rulers, authorities, and lords of this dark world, against the evil spirits that are above (Eph. 6:12).

Keep a clear head and watch! Your enemy, the devil, is prowling around like a roaring lion, looking for someone to devour (1 Peter 5:8).

Once we are on the alert, the Bible tells us how to fight the devil and all his deceptions:

Put on God's whole armor, and you will be able to stand against the devil's tricky ways (Eph. 6:11). (We suggest you also read Eph. 6:13-17).

Be strong in your faith and resist him, knowing that your fellow Christians in the world are paying the same price of suffering (1 Peter 5:9).

Then submit to God. Resist the devil and he will run away from you (James 4:7).

Don't let sin keep on using your organs as tools for doing wrong. But as people who have come back from the dead and live, give yourselves to God, and let God use your organs as tools for doing what is right (Rom. 6:13).

Friend, do not depend on yourself or on your own feelings to see you through the war between the Spirit and the flesh. Rather, depend on Christ and on the Word He has given us. He will see you through and will make you more than a conqueror. If you are on the Lord's side, you cannot lose, because He has already won *the* victory for you. When you are in Christ, you rejoice and give thanks to God for *the* victory He has given you in Christ Jesus. In the great Reformation hymn, "A Mighty Fortress Is Our God," Martin Luther addressed the same concern as you expressed in your question. He wrote:

A mighty Fortress is our God,
A trusty Shield and Weapon;
He helps us free from every need
That hath us now o'ertaken.
The old evil Foe
Now means deadly woe;
Deep guile and great might
Are his dread arms in fight;
On earth is not his equal.

With might of ours can naught be done,
Soon were our loss effected;
But for us fights the Valiant One,
Whom God Himself elected.
Ask ye, who is this?
Jesus Christ it is,
Of Sabaoth Lord,
And there's none other God;
He holds the field forever.

Though devils all the world should fill,
All eager to devour us,
We tremble not, we fear no ill,
They shall not overpower us.
This world's prince may still
Scowl fierce as he will,
He can harm us none,
He's judged; the deed is done;
One little word can fell him.

The Word they still shall let remain,
Nor any thanks have for it;
He's by our side upon the plain
With His good gifts and Spirit.
And take they our life,
Goods, fame, child, and wife,
Let these all be gone,

They yet have nothing won;
The Kingdom ours remaineth.

The Lutheran Hymnal, 262:1, 2, 3, 4

And, God, What About SEX?

And God created man in His image; in God's image He created him; He created them male and female. And God blessed them. "Have children," God told them, "and multiply and fill the earth . . ." (Gen. 1:27-28a).

This is why a man leaves his father and his mother and lives with his wife, and they become one flesh (Gen. 2:24).

From the above we can see that God intended that humans live together as husband and wife and that they have sexual relations in marriage. In other Bible passages we can read that the gift of sex is for both procreation (having children) and recreation (communicating).

It is also clear that sexual activity is solely the province of married people. Yet already in very early times the attraction of sex was so strong between people who were not married to each other that God devoted one of the Ten Commandments to the subject. We read:

Do not commit adultery (Ex. 20:14).

Today we find the same sinful sexual attraction and activities as were found at the time of Moses. This interest in sexual activity is reflected in the many questions we have received on this topic.

God's Word is clear; yet we humans try to bend or change God's design for the proper use of sex. This can be seen in the first three questions, which deal with premarital sex. The first question is from a man who claims that he is no longer bound by the rules of the church; yet his conscience tells him he is doing something wrong and he feels a need to justify his actions. The second questioner is asking if sex outside of marriage is alright when you "love" the person. The third questioner, having seen the answer to the second question, asks if you love the person and have plans for marriage, is sex outside of marriage alright? In all three questions the people are trying to find "loopholes" to justify planned or current actions. There are no "loopholes," since there is a specific time when sexual activity can begin. That time is after the marriage ceremony.

In these questions about sex, which we have grouped for convenience, we have attempted to show you how God has explained its proper use. It is our prayer that you think and live according to God's design for sex both before and after marriage.

O blessed home where man and wife
Together lead a godly life,

By deeds their faith confessing!
There many a happy day is spent,
There Jesus gladly will consent
To tarry with His blessing.

If they have given Him their heart,
The place of honor set apart
For Him each night and morrow,
Then He the storms of life will calm,
Will bring for every wound a balm,
And change to joy their sorrow.

The Lutheran Hymnal, 624:1-2

And, God, What About SEX—Premarital I?

 I am educated in the church's laws against premarital sex. At the present time I feel alienated from my religion. I still find myself with a value and morality conflict. I am engaging in premarital sex with a girl with similar upbringing. I don't feel that these actions are immoral; they are a private matter between the two loving partners. I don't know if I will ever feel sorry for these actions, and without sorrow there can be no forgiveness. Although I don't think I can feel sorry now, I might change after years. Will my attitude now and my feeling that my actions are not sinful or immoral ever prevent me from being truly regretful and thus being capable of salvation?

 We are concerned about you and your apparent unwillingness to acknowledge your sin. You cannot be saved, which means be delivered from your sinfulness and your sins and their damning consequences, unless you are really sorry that you have offended God! You cannot be saved unless you change your mind about your sinfulness and your sins. You need to change your mind from the thought that your sins are "nothing" or "not so bad," and to agree with God that they are so bad that they separate you from Him now and will do so eternally unless you are delivered from them.

You can only be saved by Jesus, for He is the only Savior there is. Please look at the question on Sorrow over SINS (page 139) for a fuller statement on the subject.

According to God's design, sex is properly used only within the bonds of holy matrimony. God did not intend for there to be such a thing as casual sex outside of marriage. It is God's intentions that there be a total-without-reservations *commitment* of a man and woman to each other. That commitment is to meet their mutual and respective responsibilities until death parts them. He expects that commitment to be made publicly "in the presence of God and witnesses." Such a total commitment is what a man and woman make to each other and to God in marriage. Sexual intercourse is the privilege of those whom God has joined together in holy wedlock. Premarital and extramarital sex are forthrightly called sin in the Bible. Such a use of sex is a violation of one of the Ten Commandments, the one that reads:

Do not commit adultery (Ex. 20:14).

Do not suppose, as some people flippantly do, that if you are not married you cannot commit adultery. The Bible clearly applies this commandment to both the married and unmarried.

Everybody should think highly of marriage and keep married life pure, because God will judge those who sin sexually whether single or married (Heb. 13:4).

The basic New Testament Greek words for sexual sin are *porno* words. In one noun form it is *pornos,* and refers to the fornicator, or the male prostitute. In another noun form it is *porne,* and refers to the fornicatrix, or the female prostitute. These words are not only used of people engaged in sex for sale; they are used of all those who abuse the God-given gift of sex. These are hard words with unpleasant implications for many people in our day.

Unfortunately, I fear you have been taken in by the relativism of our day. Relativism contends that there is nothing that is right or wrong; therefore there is no sin. This in turn means that there is no need for salvation or a Savior from sin. In place of a standard of morality, those of a relativist persuasion have substituted notions like, "If it feels good, do it," and "It's OK so long as you are loving." The anti-philosophy (Dr. Francis Schaeffer's expression) of relativism has been around for many years, and its purpose is to free modern people from guilt feelings about their past attitudes and conduct. However, people still feel guilty. They do so because they cannot shake the notion that they have not measured up to a standard of morality. The only way to resolve guilt is not by denying its existence but by recognizing it, repenting of it, and accepting the forgiveness God offers to every sinner in Christ Jesus.

Every human being alive is offered salvation. The Bible says: "God so loved the *world* . . ." (John 3:16). But frankly, we cannot accept God's forgiveness until we repent of our sins (which is really being sorry for offending God). If we do not think that we have anything to repent of, then it is obvious that we will not be able to enjoy the forgiveness, the peace, the life, and the salvation that God offers us in Christ.

In closing, permit me to challenge you to think ahead a little. Why should the girl wear a white wedding gown if she has already given herself away? Why should the girl be given away by her father if she

has already given herself away? What can "I take you ..." mean under the above circumstances? Is the vow "to be faithful in every duty," "to cleave only unto thee," really to be taken seriously from one who has used sex outside of the commitment of marriage? Given past performance, can such a one really be trusted after marriage? If premarital relations are not so bad so long as ..., then would extramarital relations be not so bad as long as ...? This challenge was not made to be unkind. It was made to encourage you to think about the consequences of your current thoughts and actions.

And, God, What About SEX—Guilt?

Yes, Cathy, despite all the rationalizations that are used, people still feel guilty. They feel guilty because they are guilty. Real moral guilt cannot be resolved by simply denying its existence. It can be resolved only through forgiveness. Such forgiveness is available to us in Jesus.

And, God, What About SEX—Premarital II?

 If you love a guy and really care about him, is it a sin to have sex with him?

 The simplest answer that can be given to your question is "yes."

In your question you seem to equate "love" with "sex," as if that alone justifies sexual intercourse. Do you love your mother and father? If so, does this love permit or suggest sex with them? Do you love your brothers and sisters? If so, does this love permit or suggest sex with them? Do you love your country or neighbor? If so, does this love permit or suggest sex? Do you love your God? Therefore, love alone does not permit or suggest a proper use of sex. Only in marriage can sex be properly used. (See the question on SEX—Premarital I.)

And, God, What About SEX—Premarital III?

 I was reading the question on page 78 (original book), and I have a related question. If a couple has premarital sex, they are in love, and they do have marriage plans, do you still apply the same answer?

 Yes.

And, God, What About SEX—Oral I?

Is oral sex a sin?

Since there are no prohibitions in the Bible against oral sex between husband and wife, this answerer would say that God would not consider such activity in marriage sinful. You should, however, recognize that a wife or husband may prefer not to participate in oral sex and may even consider it personally repugnant. Forcing the marriage partner to engage in sex in a way contrary to his or her will, scruples, and preferences can be sinful. The sin involved would be a selfishness—making one's own flesh one's god. Selfishness is definitely part of the conquest-exploitation sex syndrome that is so popular these days. Selfishness is certainly not part of the concept of commitment, love, and consideration that a man and a woman, united in holy matrimony, experience in sexual intercourse.

A husband and wife who trust in Jesus will strive, in all that they do, to "be subject to one another out of reverence for Christ" (Eph. 5:21 RSV). A Christian husband will "love his wife as Christ loved the Church" (Eph. 5:25).

You, of course, understand that male homosexuals practice oral (and anal) sex as a substitute for the female organ. Such use is clearly contrary to God's design for the proper use of sex. Such use is an abuse of sex, a perversion. Look at what God tells us about such abuse in Rom. 1:24-27 and 1 Cor. 6:9-10.

And, God, What About SEX—Oral II?

Dear Pastor, since this is a "gray area" in the Bible, what is wrong with oral sex before marriage? The previous answers didn't help much. Could you elaborate on this?

I am sorry that you were not able to make application of the previous answers to your question. Understand that this answerer does not regard your question to be in a "gray area" of the Bible.

In your question you give expression to the common notion that the only activity that can be identified as fornication is the insertion of the male penis into the female vagina by those who are not married to each other. When the Bible uses the word "fornication" in the widest sense, it applies it to all abuses of sex. On the basis of the Bible, explicit sexual activity is the privilege only of those who are committed to each other within the bonds of holy matrimony. That is God's design for the proper use of sex.

Fornication can be defined as stimulation leading to sexual climax between people who are not married to each other. It makes no difference if this stimulation is by the mouth, the hand, or actual intercourse, since the intent or purpose is the same. God does not differentiate between methods of sinning. A sin committed by thought, by word, or by deed is the same sin in the eyes of God, because He looks into the sinner's heart.

Those who think that oral sex between unmarried people is not sinful, or at least not as sinful as adultery, are looking for loopholes in what the Bible teaches is God's design for the proper use of sex. Permit me to restate what that design is. From the very beginning God intended that sex be used in the sharing of love and commitment by those He has joined together in marriage (see Gen. 2:18-25 and Eph. 5:21-33). At the end of the sixth day of creation, we read in Gen. 1:31a that

God saw that *everything* He made was very good.

That "everything" included sex, since in verse 28 God told Adam and Eve to "have children. . . ."

The Lord regards the sexual relationship between husband and wife to be so sacred that one of the Ten Commandments says:

Do not commit adultery (Ex. 20:14).

The application of this commandment throughout both the Old and New Testaments makes it very clear that anyone, not just the married, can abuse the beautiful God-given gift of sex.

We live in a world that has become obsessed with sex. Just count the number of X-rated movies, adult book stores, massage parlors, explicit sex-oriented magazines, and even the so-called sophisticated women's magazines for examples of an overt sexual orientation. This list does not even include the subtler forms of sexual exploitation on television, in newspaper advertisements, etc. This obsession with sex is a violation of the First Commandment, which says:

Do not have any other gods besides Me (Ex. 20:3).

Since sex is put before God, sex then becomes a false god moderns must turn from in order to return to "the living and true God" (1 Thess. 1:9 KJV). Those who turn from sin will want to serve the only true God by thinking and doing what He has revealed in the Bible as pleasing in His sight.

And, God, What About SEX—Masochistic?

 I wanted your opinion on this. I often enjoy pain. I like to be whipped and receive sexual gratification from it. I found this out in the most unusual way, but it is true. I will often have my sexual partner tie me up and whip me. Sometimes we will have intercourse afterwards. I often feel guilty, but it feels so good that I can't go without it. My girlfriend will perform these acts for me, but she can't understand them. Am I wrong to enjoy being whipped? Do others desire this? I have this fantasy of being whipped by a group of girls, but I don't have the guts to pursue it. Signed, Troubled But Sexually Healthy.

 I must admit that I am having difficulty taking this "question" seriously. This "question" sounds like the put-on letters sent to newspaper advice columnists.

Assuming that your question is "real," I offer the following. First, all sexual activity outside of marriage is sinful and contrary to the will of God. Second, unlike oral or anal sex, which is not forbidden to a married couple, masochistic sex is a perversion and sinful and is not permitted even to a married couple.

In my opinion, which you asked for, you are a slave to sin. If you are "for real," then you are exactly what Jesus said in John 8:34:

I tell you the truth . . . everyone who lives in sin is a slave to sin.

This Bible passage does not specifically refer to the perversion in which you have ensnared yourself, but it certainly does apply to those who abuse the beautiful gift of God which is sex. This passages applies to all who sin, which is all people. This passage points to everyone's need for liberation from sin. That liberation is provided by God for all people in Jesus. In John 8:36 Jesus said:

If, then, the Son frees you, you will really be free.

The freedom Jesus offers and effects in the lives of sinners is that which makes a person truly *untroubled* (not guilty) and spiritually *healthy* (happy). The happiness that Jesus gives is not giddiness; it is deep-seated and lasts forever. Jesus, the Son, wants to make you free. Please consider Jesus and His offer worthy of your consideration.

And, God, What About SEX—Free?

Yes, Cathy, what your "friend" claims is freedom does have "more rules than having rules does." What is called "free love" is not really free. It costs a great deal.

Jesus came right to the point when He said: "I tell you the truth . . . everyone who lives in sin is a slave to sin" (John 8:34). However, He also said: "if, then, the Son frees you, you will really be free." (John 8:36)

The freedom Jesus offers is not cheap. It cost Him a great deal. It cost Him His life.

When a person knows Jesus, the Son, then he or she is really free. That person is liberated from slavery to sin. That person is free to serve Jesus. One who loves Jesus wants to live by His Word (see John 14:15). That Word includes the rule: "Do not commit adultery" (Ex. 20:14; Mark 10:19).

And, God, What About Removing SIN from the World?

 If God has all power, why doesn't He remove sin from the world?

 Those of us who believe what God communicates to us through the Bible believe that He will do exactly what you suggest. He will do it when He uses His power to destroy all things at the end of time. That, however, is not a very happy prospect for those who are still caught in the slavery of sin.

The almighty God reveals to us in the Bible that the End has not yet come because He is patient and gracious. He delays the Day of Judgment so that sinners will have the opportunity to repent and accept the forgiveness He offers free of charge in Jesus. It is because the almighty God is also all-gracious that He does not put an end to this world, which is groaning for deliverance from the burden of sin. He is not slack about fulfilling His promises; He still sends out His message and His messengers. He still wants more and more people to join Him at the marriage supper of the Lamb. Be assured, He suffers long from the abuses perpetrated by so many people on His creatures and creation. His patience is meant to bring the perpetrators to repentance and to trust in the Savior, Jesus Christ. If God were at this very moment to use His power to remove sin from the world, all the unrepentant sinners would also be removed forever from His presence. He does not want that, nor do those who feel a burden for the souls of sinners want that.

However:

No one knows about that day or hour, not the angels in heaven, not the Son, only the Father. Be careful and watch, because you don't know when it will happen. . . . Make sure he doesn't come suddenly and find you asleep. What I tell you, I tell everyone: "Watch!" (Mark 13:32-33, 36-37).

The above answer is based on many Bible passages. You are encouraged to read and study the following Bible references, from which the answer was drawn: Luke 14:15-24; Rom. 8:21-22; 2 Peter 3:7-14; Rev. 19:7-9.

And, God, What Is Sorrow over SIN?

What exactly is sorrow for one's sins? Is it just crying and lamenting over the wrongdoings?

Sorrow for one's sins does not always involve crying and lamenting. It is certainly not "just" crying and lamenting.

The basic verb and noun for "to repent" and "repentance" (*metanoeo* and *metanoia*) are cognate words which emphasize that repentance has to do with a change of heart and mind. To be sorry for one's sins is to realize that one has disobeyed, offended, and displeased God. To repent is to realize that to continue in sin will separate one from God forever in hell. It is the law of God that comes down on us like a hammer and knocks us to our knees. Then we will pray as the sinner in the temple:

God, forgive me, a sinner! (Luke 18:13).

Repentance moves us to seek God's answer to our sins, namely forgiveness in Jesus.

There is an interesting contrast about sin and repentance in the apostle Paul's Second Letter to the Corinthians. In this passage Paul contrasts worldly grief with godly grief. Note the following:

Being sad in God's way makes you repent of sin so as to save you—you can't regret that. But the sorrow of the world brings death (2 Cor. 7:10).

Godly or good grief over one's sins is that which leads to change in one's attitude toward sin, which in turn leads to an acceptance of God's grace.

Pray with us: "O Lord, I have sinned. I am sorry for these things I have done which go against Your law. I am also sorry for not doing the things I should have done. Thank You for Your forgiveness. Please give me the strength to do Your will. I pray in Jesus' name. Amen."

And, God, What if I Am Not Sorry for My SINS?

 Is it possible to be saved if you do not really feel sorry for the sins you committed? I would be the first person to admit that I have sinned against God, and I am willing to turn from those sins. But if I am not really sorry for my sins, will He still forgive me and save me?

I am not quite clear on what you are asking or saying. If you are willing "to admit" that you have sinned against God and if you are "willing to turn from those sins," then you are by definition sorry for them. However, you say that you do not really feel sorry for them. Which is it? It cannot be both at the same time. You are either ready to admit that you are a sinner and guilty of certain sins before God, or you are not. You are either sorry for those sins, or you are not.

The most common New Testament Greek verb translated as "to repent" is *metanoeo,* which literally means "I change my mind, I change the inner man" (Alexander Souter, *A Pocket Lexicon to the Greek New Testament,* London: Oxford University Press, 1956, p. 157). The noun most commonly translated as "repentance" in the original is *metanoia,* which literally means "a change of mind, a change in the inner man" (*ibid.*). The verb is found 34 times in the New Testament, whereas the noun is found 24 times. The verb is found in such important passages as:

Repent—the kingdom of heaven is near (Matt. 3:2).

The time has come, and God's kingdom is here. Repent, and believe the good news (Mark 1:15).

. . . Because they repented when Jonah preached; and here you see more than Jonah (Luke 11:32b).

So, I tell you, there will be more joy in heaven over one sinner who repents than over ninety-nine good people who don't need to repent (Luke 15:7).

So, I tell you, God's angels will be happy over one sinner who repents (Luke 15:10).

Peter answered them, "Repent and be baptized, every one of you, in the name of Jesus Christ so that your sins will be forgiven, and you will be given the Holy Spirit" (Acts 2:38).

Repent then, and turn, to have your sins wiped out that a time may come when the Lord refreshes you . . . (Acts 3:19).
Now repent of this wickedness of yours, and ask the Lord if He will perhaps forgive you for thinking such a thing (Acts 8:22).

The noun is found in passages such as:

. . . And that repentance and forgiveness of sins should be preached in His name to all nations, beginning from Jerusalem (Luke 24:47 RSV).
For godly grief produces a repentance that leads to salvation . . . (2 Cor. 7:10a RSV).

You cannot be saved, which means be delivered from your sinfulness and your sins and their damning consequences, unless you are really sorry that you have offended God. You cannot be saved unless you change your mind about your sinfulness and your sins. You need to change your mind from the thought that your sins are "nothing" or "not so bad," and agree with God that they are so bad that they separate you from Him now and will do so eternally unless you are delivered from them.

You can only be saved by Jesus, for He is the only Savior there is. You will not accept Jesus as Savior until you recognize how damning your sins are. When you repent ("change your mind"), then God gives you a new mind; He gives you the mind of Christ. The mind of Christ submits to God's will and Word. When you have the mind of Christ, you are not perfect. Rather, you continually recognize how imperfect you are, and that leads you to daily repentance. Dr. Luther, in referring to the significance of baptizing with water in your daily life, reminds you that daily you must drown the "old man" in you so that the "new men" may daily come forth and arise. This is to remind you that repentance is not a once-and-never-again experience in the life of the Christian. Repentance, rather, is a daily thing. It can be said that the closer you draw to Christ and the deeper you sink the roots of your life into his holy Word the more sensitive you will become about your shortcomings and the more you will desire to become more like Jesus.

Don't rely too heavily on your own religious feelings or emotions. Rely, rather, on the Word of God. Take hold of it and put your trust in it. Take to heart its stern message that all have sinned, which includes you and me. But also take to heart the Bible's wonderful and comforting message that there is forgiveness with the Lord. That forgiveness is full and free in Jesus. It is offered to you and me and everyone. You can make the Good News your own when you really repent, and then trust in Jesus to deliver you for today and for all your tomorrows to eternity.

Pray with us: "Please, Lord, forgive all the sins that I have committed. I am really sorry for them. Give me the mind of Christ. Help me keep away from sin and to become more like Jesus. We ask this in the name of Jesus, Your Son and our Savior. Amen."

And, God, What About SUCCESS as the Goal of Life?

 To me, the ultimate goal in life is success—unfortunately many materialistic things come into play. Throughout my father's life, he has had to put up with corruption, graft, and other things to carry on his business. To a college student entering the working world in a few years, looking foward to this in one way or another is hard. How can I live with myself when I know I'll be a part in corruption, either corrupting myself or someone else?

 Solomon wrote:

It is better to possess a little with the fear of the Lord than have riches with turmoil (Prov. 15:16).

The greedy man brings trouble to his home, but if you refuse bribes you will live (Prov. 15:27).

A few possessions gained honestly is better than many gotten by injustice (Prov. 16:8).

Better be poor and live innocently than fat and perverse in speech (Prov. 19:1).

As you can see, corruption, graft, and materialistic success have been problems for humans for a long time. Even Cain, the firstborn of Adam and Eve, was consumed with jealousy concerning his brother's success. That jealousy led him to murder Abel (see Gen. 4:3-8).

Jesus spoke about the problem of defining success in worldly terms when He said:

Guard against every kind of greed. Even if you have more than enough, your property doesn't give you life (Luke 12:15).

A materialistic definition of success inevitably leads one into the problems you are anticipating. We are all aware of the problems a recent President of the United States became entangled in because he was willing to do anything to "succeed." Corruption, cover-ups, lies, etc., were all justified in the name of "success."

Unless you numb your conscience with the sins you describe, you will not be able to live with yourself. With a dull conscience, you'll be able to do whatever is expedient at the moment. You will make whatever means you employ seem appropriate. And, of course, in the process you will corrupt yourself and others.

You need not let that happen to you. You can resolve not to play the "success at any cost and the devil take the hindmost" game. You don't have to join the rat race and become a rat in the process. The cost, certainly, will be high. That cost may well be the loss of many of your most cherished things in this world. A clear conscience and a realization that one has not used others is worth the cost.

The proper attitude grows in the person who knows how much God loves him. Such an attitude is the work of the Holy Spirit. If you know the love of God in Christ, we urge you to get into His Word and become associated with others who really want to serve Jesus. By so doing you will be encouraged to do what is pleasing in God's sight, no matter what the earthly cost.

We pray for you and all persons engaged in corruption, graft, and other evil.

Seek the Lord while He can be found, call on Him while He is near. Every wicked man should give up his way, and every evil man what he's thinking. If he comes back to the Lord, He will be merciful to him, and to our God, He will forgive him ever so much (Is. 55:6-7).

And, God, What About SUICIDE?

What makes a person want to commit suicide? Sometimes I feel depressed and angry enough to consider it, but there is still too much to live for!

Utter despair about the meaning, purpose, and usefulness of one's life seems to be the main contributing factor leading to suicide. If a person feels that there is nothing to live for, he or she may contemplate and carry out the terrible act of suicide. Apparently it gets that bad for some people.

Indeed, there are times when we are all disappointed with the way things are going. We may be angry with others and with ourselves. We may wonder what's the use of keeping at it when things just don't seem to work out. Even though we get depressed, we should realize that when things can't get any worse the only thing that can happen is that they get better.

One who is in Christ has a great deal to live for. That person has the opportunity to serve God and others in Jesus' name. That person has the opportunity to develop talents and interests so that he or she can be a faithful steward of the many gifts God has bestowed on him or her. Even suffering for Jesus' sake gives the Christian reason for rejoicing. The Christian rejoices in suffering for Jesus because such suffering may benefit others. After a life given to faithful service to God the Christian looks forward to his Lord saying:

> Well done, good and faithful slave!... You proved you could be trusted with a little. I will put you in charge of something big. Come and be happy with your master (Matt. 25:21).
> Come, you whom My Father blessed, inherit the kingdom prepared for you from the time the world was made (Matt. 25:34).

If you have thoughts of suicide, talk to a pastor at once. He can offer you the peace that passes all understanding, which is in Christ Jesus alone. If you do not have a regular pastor, look in the Yellow Pages under "Churches" and call the nearest church, for God has assured us that when you ask, it will be given to you; when you search, you will find; when you knock [ring], the door will be opened for you (see Matt. 7:7-8).

And, God, What About the Christian Who Commits SUICIDE?

What happens to the person who had Christian teaching and Christian belief that commits suicide?

We can assume that the Christian or the person with Christian training knows that suicide is a sin. It is a sin against the commandment that reads:

Do not murder (Ex. 20:13).

This commandment applies to malicious, premeditated taking of human life. Taking one's own life would be contrary to this commandment of God. A Christian knows that sin damns and that it separates people from God. Such knowledge ordinarily moves the person in Christ to flee evil and to avoid even giving the appearance of doing evil. A Christian wants to do what is pleasing in God's sight. Obviously, suicide is not pleasing in God's sight.

We usually assume that the person who murders himself or herself does not have the opportunity to repent of the sin. No doubt some people who commit suicide have some time before they die to realize their sin and ask for forgiveness.

Repentance and remission of sins are what every sinner needs. Suicide is not the unforgivable sin, nor should it be thought of as the most heinous of sins. (See also the question of the UNFORGIVABLE Sin.) There is forgiveness with the Lord for all sins. Jesus died for all the sins of all people. The perplexing question with regard to suicide is whether the perpetrator of this crime has time to see the sin, repent of it, and turn to the Lord Jesus for remission of it. If the person who commits suicide does not have time for repentance, he or she is lost eternally, just like every other unrepentant sinner. These are hard words, but they need to be written to point out to all who read this how terrible a thing sin is. Just having Christian training is not enough. A Christian is one who trusts in the Lord Jesus and lives by faith in Him. When one does that, one is assured that no matter how difficult things get, the Lord Himself will not forsake His own.

Despite the hard words written above, this pastor feels that he can offer some consolation to the survivors of a suicide who has been "in the Lord" in life. The consolation is that somehow the person "in the Lord" was temporarily out of his or her mind and did not know that suicide was a sin. It is possible to suggest that even Christians can be so depressed that they are not aware of what they are doing. From God's side we can say that "no death or life . . . can ever separate us from God, who loves us in Christ Jesus, our Lord" (Rom. 8:38-39). This consolation of the Gospel can only be offered to the survivors of a person who in life confessed Jesus as his or her Lord and Savior and who was under the influence of the Word of God just prior to his or her death. These words are not intended to condone suicide. They are intended to stress how great the forgiveness of God is. As great as that forgiveness is, we dare not take it for granted nor should we tempt the Lord our God (see Matt. 4:5-7). The person in Christ will not want to consciously do anything that will destroy his or her faith.

And, God, What About Speaking in TONGUES?

What about tongues? Are they just an emotional thing, or something that a person draws out of his subconscious?

St. Paul talks about tongues in his First Letter to the Corinthians. (Note: In the translation quoted below, "tongues" has been translated as "another language.")

Pursue love, be eager to have the gifts of the Spirit, and especially to speak God's Word. When a man talks in another language, he doesn't talk to people but to God, because nobody understands him; his spirit is talking mysteries (1 Cor. 14:1-2).

When you talk in another language, you encourage yourself. But when you speak God's Word, you help the church grow (1 Cor. 14:4).

If I pray in another language, my spirit prays, but my mind isn't helping anyone. What then? I will pray in my spirit but also pray so as to be understood. I will sing praise in my spirit but also sing so as to be understood (1 Cor. 14:14-15).

But in a church I would rather say five words that can be understood, in order to teach others, than ten thousand words in a language nobody understands (1 Cor. 14:19).

You ask if tongues are an emotional thing. From the above we are convinced that "tongues" or "another language" is an emotional thing. It has to do with the spirit and not the mind. The words of "another language" are not intelligible unless there is an interpreter. The speaker of "another language" is only enjoying self-edification. It would seem to us that "spirit" (lower case) in this chapter could be equated with your use of the term "emotion."

Notice that St. Paul does not say we should not speak in "another language," only that we should understand that it is for the benefit of the speaker and not the listener.

You ask if tongues are drawn out of the subconscious. We regret that it is not clear to us what you mean by "subconscious." If you define the subconscious as that which is not under the control of the mind, then we would equate subconscious with spirit/emotion. We would say that tongues are drawn from the subconscious. If you have some other meaning for subconscious, we cannot give you an answer.

And, God, Does This Church Teach the One TRUE FAITH?

Should this Lutheran Student Center be considered the church for today, or the one "true church"?

We are willing to let you and God Himself judge whether our ministry is faithful to our Lord and Savior Jesus Christ. In order that you may judge wisely, we will briefly summarize what we believe, teach, and confess. We are willing to stake our claim as a "true" church on what we believe and confess.

We believe, teach, and confess that Jesus Christ is the eternal Son of God, who became a human being to seek and to save the lost. You and we were numbered among the lost. Because God so loved the world, Jesus laid down His life for us. He took our sins and the punishment we deserved because of them upon Himself. He took our sins all the way to the cross with Him. He died there in our stead. But that was not the end—He conquered death for us when He arose on the third day. Now Jesus lives, and those who trust in Him live by faith in Him.

Because we trust Jesus, we trust His Word, the Holy Bible. We believe that the Bible is the very inspired Word of God. The Bible is our only rule and norm for Christian teaching and life. We study it and believe it and will do so until Jesus comes again in glory.

You are invited to draw your own conclusion as to our faithfulness to the "apostles' doctrine" (Acts 2:42 KJV) on the basis of the answers given to theological as well as life-situation questions in this book. We want this book and all that we do here to honor God and make others wise unto the salvation available to them in Jesus.

And, God, What About the UNFORGIVABLE Sin?

Is there an unforgivable sin?

Yes, there is. Jesus calls it blasphemy* against the Holy Spirit. Read Matt. 12:31-32; Mark 3:28-29; and Luke 12:10. Blasphemy against the Holy Spirit, Jesus said, will not be forgiven because the person who does it is guilty of an eternal sin.

> . . . But anyone who talks against the Holy Spirit will not be forgiven in this world or the next (Matt. 12:32b).

But what exactly is "blasphemy against the Holy Spirit"? We can deduce certain facets of the answer from the words of Jesus in the above passages and from some verses in the epistles.

In the gospels Jesus tells us that blasphemy against the Holy Spirit is a sin in a class all by itself. He tells us that every other sin and blasphemy will be forgiven, but not blasphemy against the Holy Spirit.

In the gospels there are numerous examples of blasphemy spoken against Jesus. Early in His ministry when Jesus forgave the sins of a paralyzed man, the scribes accused Jesus of blasphemy, which was itself an act of blasphemy (see Mark 2:1-12). Late in His ministry the men who were guarding Jesus just prior to His trial before Pontius Pilate mocked, beat, and insulted (*blasphemeo* in the original) Jesus (Luke 22:63-65). Such blasphemy, Jesus said, would be forgiven to any of those who repent of their sin.

While Jesus was hanging on the cross, both of the robbers insulted Him, just as the people that passed by the site of the crucifixion did. (Matt. 27:39-44). Yet, the Spirit of God convicted one of the robbers of his sins, and he turned to Jesus and said:

Jesus, remember me when You come to Your kingdom.

And Jesus said to him:

I tell you the truth, today you will be with Me in Paradise (Luke 23:42-43).

This shows that blasphemy against Jesus is not the unforgivable sin.

The apostle Paul is another example of a person who blasphemed Jesus and was forgiven. Paul writes in 1 Tim. 1:13 that before he became a Christian he was a blasphemer and a persecutor of Jesus. Paul then confesses that Jesus had mercy on him and forgave him. This shows that neither blasphemy against Jesus nor persecution of His followers is the unforgivable sin.

In Thess. Paul urges the members of "the church of the Thessalonians which is in God the Father and the Lord Jesus Christ" (1 Thess. 1:1):

Don't put out the fire of the Spirit (1 Thess. 5:19).

This passage indicates that one who has the Spirit of God can put Him out of his or her life. When one has extinguished the fire that gives spiritual life, then he or she is dead. When such a foolish person chases the Spirit of God out of his or her life, such an action may be identified as blasphemy against the Holy Spirit.

Another Bible passage which seems related to both Jesus' statements in the gospels and Paul's admonition to the Thessalonians is found in Heb. 6:4-6:

When those who once had the light and tasted the gift from heaven, who had the Holy Spirit just as others did and tasted how good God's Word is and the powers of the coming world—when those fall away, it is impossible to bring them back to a new repentance because they to their own undoing again crucify God's Son and hold Him up for mockery.

Since it is stated in these verses that it is impossible to bring such people back from their sin, this sin is unforgivable and may be what Jesus calls blasphemy against the Holy Spirit.

Still another passage which may have a bearing on the subject of the unforgivable sin is 1 John 5:16. There the apostle John writes about a brother committing a sin that is "deadly." While John urges his fellow believers to pray that God will restore to life one who sins, he does not urge such an effort for one who has committed the "deadly" sin. Again, this passage indicates that one who is a brother or sister in Christ can fall away. Such a falling away is not ordinary sinning, but the unforgivable sin which leads to eternal death.

To summarize, anyone can blaspheme God the Father and/or God the Son. Such blasphemy is forgivable, as are other sins. But persistent, willful rejection of the Holy Spirit's work in our heart is a form of blasphemy that makes forgiveness impossible.

As a Christian do you need to worry about committing this unforgivable sin? I, along with pastors and students of the Bible before me, say "NO." We say that because he or she who is guilty of such a sin would not be the least bit worried about it. So, trust in Jesus and His Word. Pray with King David, who had sinned greatly:

Create in me a clean heart, O God, and renew a right spirit within me. Cast me not away from Thy presence, and take not Thy Holy Spirit from me. Restore unto me the joy of Thy salvation, and uphold me with Thy free Spirit (Ps. 51:10-12 KJV).

*"**Blasphemy.** Speech, thought, writing, or action manifesting irreverence toward God or anything sacred. . . . Blasphemy is to be distinguished from atheism, sacrilege, and criticism of religion. But in moral theology, it is often regarded as a sin against the virtue of religion. . . . Christians regard it as a grave or mortal sin." (Erwin L. Lueker, ed., *Lutheran Cyclopedia,* revised edition [St.Louis: Concordia Publishing House, 1975], p. 98).

And, God, What About WISDOM?

What is wisdom as extolled in the Book of Proverbs?

Wisdom in the Book of Proverbs is more than intellectual

knowledge. It is more than "accumulated philosophic or scientific learning" or "the teachings of the ancient wise men," as suggested by *Webster's Seventh New Collegiate Dictionary*. In Proverbs 9:10a we read:

> The fear of the Lord is the beginning of wisdom.

Indeed Solomon, the author of much of the Book of Proverbs, fully realized that true wisdom is given to man by God alone (see 1 Kings 4:29). Such wisdom from God is accompanied by humility on man's part (see 1 Kings 3:7). The lessons Solomon learned in his life are evident in the Book of Proverbs. However, he had a special gift from God, as reported in 1 Kings 3:2-14.

Wisdom in the Book of Proverbs is not, then, mere speculation, for it involves the whole person, his/her whole life. It has to do with God as it is reflected in a person's conduct toward others in day-to-day living. This wisdom has to do with devotional life toward God and also with attitudes toward spouse, children, neighbors, business, and even table manners. Hence, *wisdom* in the Book of Proverbs fits together with the concept of wisdom expressed elsewhere in the Old Testament. That wisdom is bound up in doing the will of God (see Deut. 4:6). The person who forsakes God's Word will forfeit real wisdom from above (see Jer. 8:8-9). The Bible calls such a person a "fool":

> A fool says in his heart, "There is no God" (Ps. 14:1a; 53:1a).

Hence, you know and grow in wisdom when you are *in* the Lord and *into* His Word.

And, God, What About WITNESSING to Christians?

In many of your sermons of late you have brought up ministering to others who are outside the sight of God. Unfortunately these people are there. The even sadder thing I see going on is our lack of ministering to our Christian brothers and sisters. Do you see this too? How are we to witness to others outside of the Spirit of God if we don't witness—through the power of the Spirit—to those who are in the sight of God?

Thank you for your reaction to some recent sermons. Such constructive criticism is always appreciated and is really more helpful than saying, "Good sermon, Pastor," or as the case may be, "Pastor, I didn't like that sermon." Your comments are helpful because they are about specifics.

It is assumed that the sermons in question were two recent ones, entitled "Are We Obligated to Win Jews for Jesus?" and "Did 'Holocaust' Sensitize You to *the* Moral Issue of Our Day?" Those sermons intentionally dealt with matters of current but also continuing concern. It was this pastor's intention to alert my brothers and sisters in Christ to today's real issues. It was also my intention to equip the hearers of those sermons with the Word of God, the sword of the Spirit, with which to fight the good fight for Jesus.

You made an astute observation when you noted that we will not be able to witness or minister to unbelievers unless we are able to witness and minister to fellow believers. Those of us who are "in Christ" need to build each other up in our trust in Him. We need to edify each other. We do that, according to 1 Cor. 14:3-4 KJV and RSV, when we "prophesy" to each other. To "prophesy" is very simply to speak the Word of God. We build each other up in Christ Jesus when we speak the Word of God to each other. Such speaking can be done in group Bible studies and when we help each other with personal problems. The very purpose for which we hold our worship services, Bible studies, and Christian coffee house is to warm each other in the *Son*. If you have not been involved in these activities, you are encouraged and invited to do so. We need all the help we can get to live for Jesus in these last days.

And, God, Isn't WITNESSING the Work of the Holy Spirit?

Q *My question deals with what was said in yesterday's sermon. We as people are not capable of witnessing; yet you say we must. Don't you believe this is the work of the Holy Spirit? Many blessings to you in Jesus.*

A Thank you for the prayer for me. May God also bless you and give you His safe speed.

Winning any person for Christ is indeed the work of the Holy Spirit. St. Paul writes in 1 Cor. 12:3:

> So I tell you, if you are moved by God's Spirit, you don't say, "Jesus is cursed," and only if you are moved by the Holy Spirit can you say, "Jesus is the Lord."

It is very clear, therefore, that the Bible teaches that no person can come to faith in Jesus by his or her own efforts. It is the Holy Spirit who raises us dead-in-sin persons to life. He convicts us of our sin, and He converts us to Christ. As a result we give *all* glory to God for our salvation in Jesus the Messiah.

However, it is also quite clear that Jesus instructs His followers:

> Go and make disciples of all people: Baptize them in the name of the Father, the Son, and the Holy Spirit, and teach them to do everything I have commanded you. And remember, I am with you always till the end of the world (Matt. 28:19-20).

Jesus has thereby instructed those of us who follow Him and call Him Lord to multiply ourselves. We are to reproduce according to our "spiritual kind."

Is there a contradiction between what the Bible tells us about the Holy Spirit creating faith in a person's heart and Jesus directing us to "make disciples"? I do not think so, because I believe that the Holy Spirit uses *earthly means* to accomplish His *heavenly ends*. We confess in the Nicene Creed that the Holy Spirit is "the Lord and Giver of Life." He gives us both physical life and spiritual life. He gives us physical life by means of our parents. He gives us spiritual life through the means of grace, which are the Word of God, Baptism, and the Lord's Supper. Thus, when the means of grace are used, people are brought to and sustained in their faith in Jesus.

Therefore you are correct when you write that it is the Holy Spirit who converts every man, woman, and child who comes to faith in Jesus. Yet the Holy Spirit works through the Word of God, when it is preached and shared. It is we who trust in Jesus now and forever who are to get the saving Word out to others. To say that conversion is the work of the Holy Spirit does not relieve us of the responsibility to be witnesses for Jesus. Just before His leave-taking (Ascension) Jesus said:

> But when the Holy Spirit comes on you, you will receive power and will testify of Me in Jerusalem, in all Judea and Samaria, and to the farthest parts of the world (Acts 1:8).

If you confess Jesus as your Lord, then the power of the Holy Spirit has come upon you. With such power you will witness for Jesus. You are filled up with Jesus and His Spirit so that you cannot do anything but share the love of God which has been poured into your heart. As such a person you know that God is so good that He loves not only you but all people. All nations need to know Jesus, the Messiah of Israel and the Savior of the world.

We urge you to pray for those who are active in the mission activities of the church. We urge you to talk about your faith to fellow Christians. We urge you to talk about Jesus to your friends who are not Christians. Speak with them about your concern for all people and their need to learn about the Savior.

Pray with us: "O God, through the grace of Your Holy Spirit You pour the gifts of charity into the hearts of Your faithful people. Grant us health, both of mind and body, that we may love You with our total strength and with our whole heart witness in a way that is pleasing to You; through Jesus Christ, Your Son, our Lord. Amen."

And, God, What About Good WORKS?

Q *I have heard it said that unbelievers cannot do good works. Is that so?*

A Jesus the Savior said:

I am the Vine, you are the branches. If you stay in Me and I in you, you can bear much fruit; for without Me you can do nothing (John 15:5).

In this passage Jesus speaks about the results that come from the union of Vine and branches. The branches produce fruit, much fruit. Conversely, the branch that is not connected to the Vine cannot produce any fruit. Jesus tells us that one who does not abide in Christ can do *nothing*. The difficult-to-take conclusion, then, must be that if you are not a branch of Christ, the True Vine, you can "do nothing" in the sight of God. These simple words of Jesus tell us that the unbeliever is not able to do good works in the sight of God.

The writer of the Epistle to the Hebrews repeats the essence of Jesus' statement when he writes:

But you can't please God without faith (Heb. 11:6).

An unbeliever is one who does not possess faith or trust in Jesus as Savior. Without the basic trust in Jesus for the forgiveness of all his or her sin, no person can do anything that pleases God.

That written, I hasten to add that it is possible for unbelievers to be very good and moral people. Unbelievers are capable of what are called works of civil righteousness. All people are expected to obey the governing authorities. Such governing authorities have been instituted by God. They serve as agents of God to maintain order in the world (see Rom. 13:1-7). Unbelievers as well as believers are to obey such governing authorities and the laws they establish for civil order. Paying taxes, obeying traffic regulations, casting one's ballot, etc., may be considered civil good works, but such good works do not have eternal value before God in heaven.

The Christian does not do good works in order to earn salvation. The Christian does good works as the fruit of trust in Jesus. The Christian is one who lives by faith in Jesus, and who knows:

> Blessed are the dead who die in the Lord from now on. "Yes," says the Spirit, "they will rest from their labor, for their deeds will follow them" (Rev. 14:13 NIV).

Note that the deeds or the good works of people do not go before them as their "ticket" into heaven. Good works follow them. One's blessedness is dependent upon being "in the Lord." We are in the Lord when we believe in Jesus Christ. Then,

> Anyone who lives in the truth comes to the Light so that his works may be seen to have been done in God (John 3:21).

And, God, What About WORRYING?

What can you do to stop worrying? Not concern, but unnecessary worry. Please give me the right answer so I can beat this sin of the devil. I want to beat this so bad I can't describe it. It's the only thing that's holding my life back. Also Christian life. Please give me an answer so I can beat this. Me and Jesus.

The best solution to the problem of worry is found in the invitation of God in 1 Peter 5:7, which reads:

> Throw all your worry on Him because He takes care of you.

Those are wonderful words. Notice how comprehensive they are; God invites us to unload *all* our worries on Him. We can be certain that those worries and anxieties we give to God will not be given back to us. God is the Giver of only good and perfect gifts.

I believe that the Bible is the very Word of God. It has been given to us to make us wise unto salvation and to equip us to live for God. I am confident that when we appreciate the meaning of such passages as 1 Peter 5:7 we can avail ourselves of the help God would give us in every circumstance of life. God never promised us a rose garden while we follow Jesus. In fact, Jesus makes it quite clear that those who follow

Him will encounter troubles that the unbeliever does not encounter. It is when we are in the middle of ordinary human troubles as well as the special troubles that beset Christians in this sinful world that we need to bring to our remembrance words of God such as the following:

> Call Me in time of trouble! When I rescue you, you should honor me (Ps. 50:15).
> Trust the Lord with all your heart, and don't depend on your own understanding. Acknowledge Him in everything you do, and he will make your paths smooth. Don't think you are wise. Fear the Lord and turn away from evil (Prov. 3:5-7).
> Come to Me, all you who are working hard and carrying a heavy load, and I will give you rest (Matt. 11:28).
> Finally, let the Lord and His mighty power make you strong. Put on God's whole armor, and you will be able to stand against the devil's tricky ways (Eph. 6:10-11; read the remainder of the chapter).
> Let us not stay away from our worship services, as some are regularly doing, but let us encourage one another, all the more because you see the day coming nearer (Heb. 10:25).
> Then don't lose your courage. There's a great reward for it. You need endurance to do what God wants and so to get what He promised (Heb. 10:35-36).

The above passages direct you to trust in God, to speak to Him in prayer, to take advantage of the blessing and fellowship He offers. Such activities are the opposite of worry.

I must comment on your statement, "It's the only thing that's holding my life back." There is no *one* thing that can hold you back, for as soon as you get rid of one thing a new one (or two) arrives to take its place. We must rely on God's promise that He will give us the strength to withstand *all* temptation. Even Paul was not able to get rid of the one thing he felt was holding him back (see 2 Cor. 12:7-10). Yet, with the strength the Holy Spirit gave, we know what great things Paul accomplished. Now, do not give up; do not stop trying to improve yourself; do not say, "I am what I am and I cannot change." I am only suggesting that to blame *one* thing for all your problems is not realistic.

My prayer for you is the common benediction:

> The Lord bless you and keep you! The Lord let His face shine upon you and be merciful to you! The Lord look kindly at you and give you *peace!* (Num. 7:24-26).

Index of Bible Passages